Precision Construction

*Principles, Practices and
Solutions for the
Internet of Things in Construction*

Timothy Chou
A. Vincent Vasquez

Co-Storytellers

Gordon McDonald

Shawna Ermold

Mike Bierschbach

Chris Hummel

Helge Jacobsen

Steve Lineberry

Sam Hassan

Doug Seven

Chris Hulsey

Guru Bandekar

Tim Truex

Gary Burgess

Keith Gelinas

Tim Streightiff

Mike Berrisford

Nate Baldwin

Zak Podkaminer

Matt Gallien

Paul Sellis

Keith Kramlich

Burcin Kaplanoglu, PhD

Krishna Madhuvarsu

Precision Construction

*Principles, Practices and
Solutions for the
Internet of Things in Construction*

Timothy Chou
A. Vincent Vasquez

PRECISIONSTORY

http://www.precisionstory.com

ISBN 978-0-692-17096-0
Printed in the United States of America
Version 1.0, Build 22

Precision Construction — The Movie

Receive a complimentary subscription
To Precision Construction movies and shows
By visiting:

http://www.precisionstory.com

Foreword

Over the past twenty-five years, productivity has become the golden ring across industries, with varying degrees of success. Today, productivity is both an operational goalpost and a path to better customer service.

From my own vantage point of equipment rental—an industry where I've spent my entire career—the two largest markets we serve are the construction and industrial sectors. Interestingly, they've had markedly different success with productivity gains. According to a 2017 McKinsey analysis[1], the global manufacturing industry—a lynchpin of the industrial sector—has nearly doubled its productivity since 1995, while construction productivity has more or less remained flat.

So, what can be done about it? Understand the lessons from other businesses and sectors that have harnessed the power of digital connectivity. There's no inherent reason why the construction process should be any different. The job-site data collected through machine connectivity leads to more precise operations and better agility. This may require a change in perspective, but my personal experience is that contractors welcome any technology that has a track record of productivity improvements.

Electrification and autonomous operation are two examples of data-driven trends that can prepare the construction industry for the future, just as they're shaping transportation. On construction sites, unforeseen obstacles are frequently the norm, making real-time information a major defense against waste and risk. In addition to

---

[1] The Construction Industry's Productivity Problem
https://www.economist.com/leaders/2017/08/17/the-construction-industrys-productivity-problem

business intelligence, the environmental benefits of electric vehicles and the cost benefits of autonomous operation are universally attractive.

In the manufacturing sector, the automation of repetition has long dominated productivity and is now being supercharged by artificial intelligence. Similar tactics have a place in construction. Architects are rethinking how buildings are designed, and contractors are rethinking how to build them. Equipment manufacturers are developing ever-smarter machines that reduce risk and shoulder the more routine aspects of construction.

In each of these areas, safety continues to be of paramount importance. We now have the ability to digitally monitor the safety of construction workers on job sites. We can arm them with advanced software tools that rival those used in white-collar offices. The implications of the Internet of Things, including augmented reality and voice-activation, are just now being explored in the construction space. It's clear that the job site of the future will look dramatically different.

And finally, the buildings we live and work in will get smarter in ways that improve our quality of life. Digital sensors will ensure the quality of our air and water. People will move around inside a building—physically and virtually—using new technologies, and the buildings themselves will be much more proactive in consuming resources. Intelligent machines will protect us from natural disasters, theft and other threats, while self-learning from each incident.

There's an exciting road of innovation ahead for the construction industry. Precision Construction offers a glimpse of this data-powered world that's opening up for buyers, sellers, renters and users of construction equipment. I hope you'll take note and join me in supporting the industry's evolution to a new level of productivity and safety.

Matthew J. Flannery
President and Chief Operating Officer, United Rentals
November 2018

Contents

Co-Storytellers ii

Foreword x

Acknowledgements xx

Preface xxii

Part 1: Principles and Practices 1

1. Introduction - Principles and Practices 3

Economics 4

Not Internet of People 5

Next-Generation Enterprise Software 6

Internet of Things 7

2. Framework 9

IoT Framework 10

Build Machines 12

Not Machine Builder 14

Industry 17

Summary 17

3. Things Principles 19

Sensors 20

Computer Architecture 21

Software 22

Security 24

Standards 25

Packaging 27

4. Things in Practice 29

Track Loaders 29

Boom Lifts 30

Retrofitting Existing Equipment 31

Engines 33

Diesel Generators 34

Environmental Monitors 34

Robotics 36

Augmented Reality Glasses 37

Next...39

5. Connect Principles..41
Networking Fundamentals...41
Data-Link Layer...43
Range vs. Power...43
Range vs. Data Rate..45
Application Layer...46
Network Security..48

6. Connect in Practice...51
Cellular Network..51
WiFi...53
Satellite..54
Zigbee...55
LoRaWAN..55
Firewalls..57
Next..59

7. Collect Principles...61
SQL RDBMS..62
NoSQL...63
Time Series..64
Heterogeneous Data...66
Cloud Computing...68

8. Collect in Practice 71
United Rentals..72
Precision Contractor...73
JLG..74
Takeuchi...75
Skanska...75
Oracle..76
Next..76

9. Learn Principles..79
Database Query...80
Prediction..81
Novelty Detection..82

Clustering..84

Dynamic Machine Learning..85

Learning Lifecycle 86

10. Learn in Practice..91

Lead Time and Delivery...92

Location and History Mapping 92

Utilization vs. Performance Benchmarks.......................93

Alerts and Notifications 93

The Human Element to Utilization 94

Geo-fencing 94

Service Calls 94

Machine Failure..95

Operations and Regeneration 96

Analytics Tools...97

Next...98

11. Do Principles..101

Enterprise Applications 102

Middleware...102

Precision Machines: Improved Quality of Service...........103

Precision Machines: Reduced Cost of Service 104

Precision Machines: New Business Models...................105

Software-Defined Machine 106

Business Model 1: Product and Disconnected Services..........106

Business Model 2: Product and Connected Services 108

Business Model 3: Product-as-a-Service......................109

Chief Digital Services Officer......................................109

Precision Service: Lower Consumables Cost 111

Precision Service: Higher Quality Product or Service.........111

Precision Service: Improved Health and Safety 112

Summary 112

12. Do in Practice..115

Precision Machines 116

Precision Contractors 118

Packaged IoP Applications...122

Next-Generation Middleware 123

13. Summary - Principles and Practices **125**

Part 2: Solutions **131**

14. Introduction - Solutions **133**

15. Precision United Rentals **139**

Things 140

Connect 144

Collect 144

Learn 145

Do 151

Summary 154

16. Precision Solar Energy Project **157**

Things 158

Connect 160

Collect 160

Learn 161

    KPI: Lead Time and Delivery Performance 161

    KPI: Service Calls 162

    KPI: Equipment Exchanges 163

    KPI: Utilization Performance vs. Benchmark 164

Do 165

17. Precision Contractor **167**

Things 168

Connect 169

Collect 170

Learn 171

Do 171

Summary 174

18. Precision Scissor and Boom Lifts **177**

Things 178

Connect 181

Collect 181

Learn 182

Do 183

Summary 185

19. Precision Track Loaders 187
Things 188
Connect...190
Collect 191
Learn 191
Do...195
Summary 196

20. Precision Environmental Monitoring.............199
Things 201
Connect...205
Collect 206
Learn 207
Do...209
Summary 210

21. Precision Construction with Augmented Reality 213
Things 216
Connect...217
Collect 218
Learn 219
Do...223
Summary 226

22. Precision Robotic Masonry 227
Things 229
Connect...233
Collect 233
Learn 234
Do...236
Summary 239

23. Summary - Solutions 241
Service Economy..244

Glossary of Terms 249
Index of Vendors 261
Index of Terms...267

Figures

Figure 2.1: IoT Framework 10

Figure 2.2: GE IoT Framework 13

Figure 2.3: PTC IoT Framework 16

Figure 5.1: OSI Model..42

Figure 5.2: Range vs. Power...44

Figure 5.3: Range vs. Data Rate 45

Figure 5.4: Size of Antenna..46

Figure 5.5: Application Layer 47

Figure 6.1: Connection Security..58

Figure 9.1: CRISP (Data Mining) Lifecycle 87

Figure 14.1: Precision Framework 134

Figure 15.1: Portable "Slap Track" Device 141

Figure 15.2: Retrofit Device..142

Figure 15.3: M8 Advanced Monitoring Device 143

Figure 15.4: UR Equipment on Rent with GPS 145

Figure 15.5: Mapping Equipment..146

Figure 15.6: History Mapping 147

Figure 15.7: Utilization from Mapping 148

Figure 15.8: Consumption Management with Alerts 149

Figure 15.9: Geo-fencing...150

Figure 15.10: Visibility provided by Total Control® Mobile..........151

Figure 16.1: On time Delivery Example 161

Figure 16.2: Equipment Exchanges Example 163

Figure 16.3: Example Utilization Performance versus Benchmark .163

Figure 18.1: JLG Boom Lift   and Scissor Lift...............................178

Figure 18.2: JLG Standard Four-Pin Telematics-Ready Plug..........180

Figure 18.3: ClearSky Dashboard 182

Figure 19.1: TL12V2 Track Loader 189

Figure 19.2: ZTR M8HZT..189

Figure 19.3: TFM user interface–map 192

Figure 20.1: Traditional Jobsite Environmental Monitoring............200

Figure 20.2: Hackathon Whiteboard Brainstorming 202

Figure 20.3: inSite Monitor Modular Design 203

Figure 20.4: inSite Monitor Solution High-Level Architecture 205

Figure 20.5: inSite Monitor Mobile App...208

Figure 21.1: Design Tech High School 215

Figure 21.2: DAQRI Smart Glasses™ 216

Figure 21.3: Show Application..220

Figure 21.4: Tag Application 221

Figure 22.1: SAM100...229

Figure 22.2: Definitions..230

Figure 22.3: SAM Robot at Work 232

Figure 22.4: Day Overview Dashboard...234

Figure 22.5: Two-Day Summary...234

Figure 22.6: SAM at Work on a Tall Building...................................235

Figure 22.7: SAM and Mason Working Together..............................237

Figure 22.8: A Brick Wall Built by SAM 238

Acknowledgements

We wanted to write a book that gave the reader a useful, conceptual framework to think about the coming generation of connected construction machines—one that is practical, not metaphorical. Much of that practical information comes from real cases of what innovative people are doing in the field.

That said, we'd like to begin by thanking our co-storytellers. Representing a core group of individuals who are leading the innovation in the field, these subject matter experts contributed their deep knowledge of how the Internet of Things is reshaping the construction industry.

In particular, we'd like to thank the leaders at United Rentals: Helge Jacobsen, Gordon McDonald, Mike Bierschbach and Chris Hummel, as well as Sam Hassan from ZTR Control Systems, as they were involved with this project from the beginning providing guidance on the book's overall direction.

In addition, we'd like to thank Shawna Ermold from United Rentals, Matt Gallien from ZTR Control Systems; Steve Lineberry, Riki Adams, Michael Iacovella and Jennifer Brewer from Skanska; Doug Seven, Lisa Watlington, Steve House and Brian Cope from Microsoft; David Caldwell, Keith Kramlich and Jonathan Martinez from Takeuchi; Jaco du Plessis and Chris Hulsey from TALISMAN Rentals; Tim Truex from Kokosing Construction; Guru Bandekar, Jonathan Dawley and Tim Streightiff from JLG; Keith Gelinas from ORBCOMM; Zak Podkaminer from Construction Robotics; Mike Berrisford from F.A. Wilhelm Construction Company; Paul Sells from DAQRI; Nate Baldwin formally from DAQRI; Judi Palmer, Burcin Kaplanoglu and Suresh Madhuvarsu from Oracle.

Writing a book requires a lot of one's time. Vince would like to thank his wife, Brenda, and their two boys, Diego and Dax, for always being supportive and giving him the time over the years to roll up his sleeves to dive into learning. Vince would also like to thank his (late) mother, Trudy, and father, Tony, for instilling in him a work ethic and expectation that it's okay to question the status quo.

Timothy would like to thank his wife, Sue, and three daughters, Danielle, Alexandra and Caroline, for always supporting him and giving him the time to learn, teach and do many things over the years. He'd also like to thank his parents, David Yuan-Pin and Mary Ann Mei-En Chou, who were both teachers and, whether by genetics or environment, inspired him to try to understand the world well enough to explain it to others.

Preface

In the world of construction equipment suppliers, including both manufacturers (OEMs) and rental agencies, no one is asking why they should invest in the Internet of Things (IoT), or what we often refer to as *telematics*. None of these players are asking why they should invest in adding software and connectivity to their machines so that data can be obtained about both their internal state and external operating environments. No one is asking why it's important to invest in cloud-based analytics tools that will help them to learn and derive insights from the data coming off machines in the field. And even for those who don't completely understand all the reasons why, they do know it's a connected world and they need to do something.

Rather than asking *why*, the question on everyone's mind is *how*? OEMs and rental agencies are asking about business models: How do I bring to market a new set of service offerings enabled by this next generation of connected machines and cloud-based analytics tools when my customers are accustomed to thinking of a service contract as "break-fix"? As a customer, why should I pay for service when the machine I purchase or rent is supposed to just work? How can I utilize my new services to build customer loyalty? How do I technically build and bring to market this new suite of services to ultimately help customers increase productivity and safety at the job site?

As an example, United Rentals was initially laser focused on providing equipment run hours and location. Today, they are way beyond bringing to market this basic, core offering and are looking at this opportunity on a much broader scale. United Rentals knows that helping customers rent only the equipment they truly need for only the duration required to get the job done will save customers money and thereby build loyalty.

Things are different on the consumption side. Of course, there are market leaders like Kokosing Construction and Black & Veatch, but many of the stakeholders rolling up their sleeves at the construction sites are still skeptical about this technology, wondering if it will truly make their lives easier and help them complete projects on time and under budget. Status quo can be a powerful deterrent to change.

In this new, IoT, telematics-enabled world, the field foreman—already working with very thin margins—can put away his clipboard and utilize his mobile device to gain real-time access to the location of his equipment and know what is in operation and what's not. The purchasing agent—who was previously tasked with buying and renting equipment without knowing what was happening at the job site—now gains real-time visibility into equipment utilization and can check against established benchmarks, all while ensuring that her equipment suppliers are meeting their obligations. And the overall executive, such as the CEO, CFO or head of operations—who previously never cared about equipment—is now given a way to shave costs and feel more in control of the money being spent through improved equipment management. And this is just the beginning.

Regardless of whether you're a supplier or consumer of construction machines, understanding how to capitalize on telematics and the Internet of Things can be confusing at best. Precision Construction was built to help demystify this complicated topic, starting with a description of the Precision Framework (Things, Connect, Collect, Learn, Do) and moving into a number of real-world examples from the construction industry, organized and told using that framework.

Not Metaphorical

The focus of this book is not metaphorical; it's practical. We try to explain all of the acronyms and use them in such a way that you'll be able to talk about these topics with others in the field. The audience for this book is business people who need to understand the technology, as well as technology people who need an introduction to the domain of construction. *Precision Construction* was written to validate why leaders need to continue to invest in telematics and provides insights into how to go about it.

Not Just the Facts

While there will be plenty of specific facts, it's also important to meet some of the characters who are pioneering IoT applications and understand some of their stories. We include a number of stories that discuss how Things from track loaders and boom lifts to robots and augmented reality glasses are being deployed by market leaders at the job site. In a fast-moving industry, it's important to understand what some of the other tribes have done.

Not Technology-Vendor Centric

This book does not tell the story from one vendor's point of view. We've created a vendor-neutral framework and you'll see how more than one hundred companies are contributing.

Not Fragmented

As you will see, IoT applications can be complex and span many domains. Rather than focusing deeply on one particular area (say, connecting Things), this book gives a complete picture.

In fact, *digital transformation* is much more than a grouping of two buzzwords. Every industry is en route to becoming digital, including the construction industry. The laggards in this transformation are at risk of being left behind, or worse yet, perishing to the players that understood the importance in advance. Precision Construction provides a pragmatic roadmap for those who are just getting started as well as those who have already begun their IoT/telematics journey.

That said, this book is also written for students, young and old. Dr. Chou teaches at Stanford University, but has also delivered guest lectures at a number of universities such as MIT, Columbia, Northwestern, Rice and UC Berkeley. When talking to these students he sees a group of people who are uninterested in building the next social network or dating site, but instead want to put their talents to work for something greater.

Finally, as we'll discuss later in more detail, the developing economies of the world—South East Asia, Latin America and Africa—will fuel global economic development as their populations grow, but also require a first-world infrastructure in industries such as power, water and healthcare. Do you think this will happen the same old way or will technology play a hand?

Part 1: Principles and Practices

1

Introduction – Principles and Practices

Many people think the Internet of Things is about your toaster talking to your refrigerator. While there will no doubt one day be very useful consumer IoT applications, the focus here is on applications of the enterprise IoT. This is a practical guide to a complete, vendor-agnostic framework for business and technology professionals. Enterprise IoT applications are complex and without a framework it can be difficult to separate hype from reality. For each of the five layers of the framework—Things, Connect, Collect, Learn, Do—we'll cover a handful of key principles that are important today and in the future. As a practical guide, we also want to make sure you understand how these principles are used in practice today. Finally, we'll put all five layers together and take you through current cases of building precision machines and the impact those might have on modern infrastructure: power, water, agriculture, transportation and healthcare.

Economics

Before we get started it's important to understand that the opportunity to build precision Things and operate them more precisely is being made possible because of fundamental shifts in the economics of computing.

The move of enterprise applications (e.g., financial, sales, marketing, purchasing, payroll, human resource management) to the cloud has been driven by an order of magnitude shift in economics. This is because the true cost of enterprise applications is not the purchase price, but instead the cost to manage the security, availability, performance and change in the application and all of the supporting hardware and software. A simple rule of thumb is that the cost to manage an enterprise application is four times the purchase price per year, which means in four years you'll spend 16 times the purchase price to manage the application. The fundamental cost component to manage the application is human labor. While finding lower labor rate countries has resulted in some decreases in cost, there is a floor.

Enterprise application cloud services are significantly lower cost because they have standardized their processes and infrastructure, and automated the management of security, availability, performance and change, thereby replacing human labor with computers. This same principle is now being applied to compute and storage infrastructure, resulting in dramatically lower costs and increased flexibility.

Dr. Chou started teaching a class on cloud computing at Tsinghua University in China a few years ago. To help with the class, the Amazon Web Services (AWS) team kindly donated $3,000 worth of compute time. At the time, that would buy a small server in Northern Virginia for 3.5 years, which interestingly didn't get any of the students excited. On the other hand, $3,000 would also buy 10,000 computers for 30 minutes, which got everybody thinking.

Not Internet of People

Most first and second-generation enterprise software was focused on us—people, individuals or groups. People in the enterprise software space had to do this because these applications had to do something useful, like help us buy a book, issue a purchase order, recruit more employees or communicate with others.

But Things aren't people. This may seem obvious, but let's discuss three fundamental differences.

More Things Than People
These days, you can't be on the internet without seeing some pronouncement about how many Things are going to become connected. John Chambers, former CEO of Cisco, recently declared there will be 500 billion Things connected by 2024. That's nearly 100 times the number of people on the planet.

Things Tell You More Than People
The main mechanism people use to tell applications something is a keyboard, and most applications use some kind of form to collect simple amounts of data from each of us. But Things have many more sensors; a typical cell phone has nearly 14 sensors, including an

accelerometer, GPS and even a radiation detector. Industrial Things like wind turbines, gene sequencers or high-speed inserters can easily have 100 sensors.

Things Talk Constantly
Most of the data from Internet of People (IoP) applications comes from either encouraging us to buy something or making it part of the hiring process. In short, people don't enter data frequently into an ecommerce, human resources (HR), purchasing, customer relationship management (CRM) or enterprise resource planning (ERP) application. On the other hand, a utility grid power sensor can send data 60 times per second, a construction forklift once per minute, and a high-speed inserter once every two seconds.

Things aren't people.

Next-Generation Enterprise Software

The first generation of enterprise application software from SAP, Oracle, Siebel, PeopleSoft and Microsoft leveraged the availability of low-cost, client-server computing to automate key financial, HR, supply chain and purchasing processes. The business model was based on licensing the application software with the purchasing company left with the responsibility (and cost) of managing the security, availability, performance and change in the software.

In 2000, the second generation of enterprise application software began. It was largely differentiated by a fundamental shift in the delivery model where the software provider took on the responsibility of managing the software. And with that change also came a change to the business model. Rather than an upfront licensing fee, a software-as-a-service (SaaS) model emerged, which allowed customers to purchase the service monthly or annually. You've probably heard of many suppliers from this era including Salesforce.com, WebEx, Taleo, SuccessFactors, NetSuite, Vocus, Constant Contact and Workday, to name a few.

As a result, most of the basic functions—sales, marketing, purchasing, hiring, benefits, accounting—have been automated. While you can debate effectiveness, it's largely a solved problem; however, while these improvements in operational efficiency through CRM or ERP software are good, they're hardly transformative. It's really only in the areas of retail (think Amazon) and banking (think eTrade and PayPal) that software has transformed business.

Perhaps now, with the changing economics of computing, the continued innovations in communications technology and decreasing cost of sensors, we can move to the third generation of enterprise software and tackle the challenges of precision agriculture, power, water, healthcare and transportation, and fundamentally reshape businesses and our environment.

Internet of Things

IoT has somewhat become like the old story of the blind men and the elephant, where each man touches a different, single part of the elephant and therefore have different versions of what the elephant *is*. Meaning, many people have differing ideas of what IoT exactly is. In this book we're going to establish a framework (with examples) that covers all of the major components of IoT applications. It's a five-layer, vendor-neutral framework that can be used by both technical and business people.

Given this framework, Part 1 is composed of chapter pairs—principles and practices—for each layer. The principle chapters are meant to describe fundamental technology principles. If you're an expert in machine learning or networking, these chapters will seem trivial. They are meant to give the reader an introduction to a handful of fundamental principles that are the foundation of technical products particularly relevant to IoT. Each of the five principle chapters is paired with a chapter on practices. In these chapters you'll see specific use cases which will illustrate some of the fundamental principles in practice.

In Part 2 we highlight a series of case studies that share examples of how IoT is being deployed and consumed across many of the potential stakeholders. For instance, we have cases that highlight contractors, rental agencies, OEMs and IoT solution development. We also highlight a few emerging technologies that are starting to impact construction with augmented reality and robotics. By using precision technologies, manufacturers can build precision machines, which will allow them to deliver better service at a lower cost and, in some cases, fundamentally transform their business models. Those who are users of these new precision machines will be able to reduce their operating costs, increase the quality of their service, and in many cases, increase worker health and safety. In a world that is increasing in population and also trying to increase the standard of living, operating a more precise planet will be paramount.

Let's get started on the journey.

2

IoT Framework

Whether you're building, buying, selling or investing in technology to enable enterprise IoT applications, it's important to utilize a framework that you can use to understand the various components or parts of the industry. Furthermore, business and technology people should understand the framework. And finally, while there are players who would like to provide many parts of the solution, it's valuable to have a vendor-independent framework.

In this chapter we'll focus on defining the various parts of an IoT framework, which is composed of five layers: Things, Connect, Collect, Learn and Do. We'll then take a few of the companies that are providing several of these components and map them to the framework. Of course, these will not be the only products we'll highlight.

IoT Framework

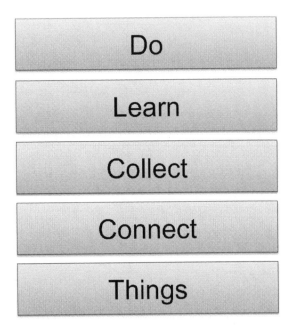

Figure 2.1: IoT Framework

The first layer is Things (the terms *Thing, machine* and *equipment* are used interchangeably), focusing on the machines themselves, which are connected to the internet in many different ways. Once connected, Collect refers to the technologies designed to collect the data, which are increasingly time-series data being sent every hour, minute or second. The fourth layer is Learn. Unlike in the world of IoP applications that had to entice you to type something, IoT applications will get data constantly, enabling us to learn from our Things for the first time. Finally, what's all this technology for? What are the business outcomes? The Do layer describes both the software application technologies and the business models that impact companies that build Things, as well as those who use them to deliver things like healthcare, transportation or construction services.

Things

Enterprise Things, whether that's a gene sequencer, locomotive or water chiller, are becoming smarter and more connected. If you're going to build or buy next-generation machines, you'll need to consider sensors, CPU architectures, operating systems, packaging and security. Sensors are beginning to follow Moore's Law, becoming dramatically lower in cost every year. These sensors are increasingly attached to low-cost computers, which can range from simple microcontrollers to fully featured CPUs supporting either the ARM or Intel instruction set architecture. As you move to more powerful processors, more powerful software can be supported, and that software becomes the point of vulnerability in an increasingly hostile world.

Connect

Things can be connected to the internet in a variety of ways and doing so requires a diverse set of technologies based on the amount of data that needs to be transmitted, how far it needs to go, and how much power you have. Furthermore, you have many choices at a higher level on how to manage the connection and how it's protected and secured.

Collect

Things aren't people. The sheer volume of data that can be generated by Things will be exponentially larger than that of IoP applications. Data might be collected and stored using SQL, NoSQL, traditional time-series, and next-generation, time-series collection architectures.

Learn

With an increasing amount of data coming from Things, we'll need to apply technology to learn from that data. Learning and analysis products will include query technology and both supervised and unsupervised machine-learning technologies. Because, as an industry, we have mostly focused on IoP applications, most of the technology applied to learning from data streams has been applied to learning from data about people. As with all parts of the stack, there is room for future innovation.

Do

As it was with IoP applications, there will be both packaged applications (e.g., ERP, CRM) and middleware to build IoT applications. Of course, these applications—whether bought or built—have to ultimately drive business outcomes. As machines become increasingly complex and enabled by software, many of the lessons learned in software maintenance and service will also apply to a machine service. As many in software already know, the movement to delivering software as a service has revolutionized the industry.

To attach the framework to real products, we'll use five suppliers who provide many (but not all) of the components of the IoT framework, with the objective to illustrate some of the similarities and differences.

Build Machines

When General Electric (GE) Vice Chairman, Daniel Heintzelman, delivered a guest lecture to Dr. Chou's Stanford class, he discussed the impact that former GE Chairman and CEO, Jack Welch, had on the company. What you may not know is how Welch was integral in moving GE from being just a provider of machines (like jet engines), to providing service contracts on those machines. That focus resulted in GE selling service contracts valued at nearly $50 billion in 2014, ending that year with about $189 billion in multi-year service agreements.

Realizing that service is powered by software and information, current GE CEO, Jeff Immelt, took another big step in 2011 and hired William (Bill) Ruh to lead a significant investment in software. Headquartered in San Ramon, CA, this software group developed Predix, a platform for building industrial IoT applications.

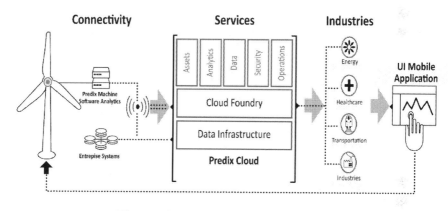

Figure 2.2: GE IoT Framework

Unlike a traditional software company, GE builds machines, such as its new gas turbine, which weighs over 400 tons, has 3,000 sensors, and generates enough electricity to power 400,000 homes.

But now GE also builds software. For instance, Predix Machine is GE's device-independent software stack to **connect** machines to the internet; it brings data from various sensors and devices into the Predix Cloud. Data is **collect**ed by Predix Data Services, which provides time-series service, as well as an enterprise SQL-on-

Hadoop analytic engine. **Learn**ing is implemented by Predix Analytics Services, which provides a framework for developing and embedding advanced analyses in business operations. Some middleware services such as Predix Security Services and a UI builder are also made available. Finally, one of the things you can **do** with the data is asset, thing and machine modeling; the Predix Asset Service enables application developers to create and store assets. For example, a developer can create an asset model that describes the logical component structure of all pumps in an organization, and then create instances of that model to represent each pump.

There are a group of companies like GE (e.g., Bosch and Schneider Electric) that also build Things and are taking steps to power machines with software and provide their software to others.

Not Machine Builder

PTC is an example of a company that does not build machines. PTC has built a one-billion-dollar business in two major areas: Computer Aided Design (CAD) and Product Lifecycle Management (PLM). With almost 250,000 CAD application subscribers and 1.6 million PLM application subscribers, the revenues are almost evenly split. To fuel growth, PTC has focused heavily on IoT software, and given their existing customer base, they have a distinct advantage in the ability to bring products to the market. Recently, the PTC CFO said they are targeting over $50 million in sales, but more importantly, 40% growth. Sterling Auty of JP Morgan Chase says, "The subscription transition trend reemerged, and in fact our favorite stock for 2016 is PTC, a name that is undergoing a transition, but will also benefit from the fast growth, secular trend in IoT."

In Harvard Business Review's November 2014 article "How Smart, Connected Products Are Transforming Competition," Harvard professor and PTC board member, Michael Porter, and PTC CEO, Jim Heppelman, discussed PTC's vision and the ten new strategic choices facing companies in this new competitive landscape. They concluded by writing:

> *"Smart, connected products are changing how value is created for the customers, how companies compete, and the boundaries of competition itself. These shifts will affect virtually every industry, directly or indirectly. But smart, connected products will have a broader impact than this. They will affect the trajectory of the overall economy, giving rise to the next era of IT-driven productivity growth for companies, their customers, and the global economy."*

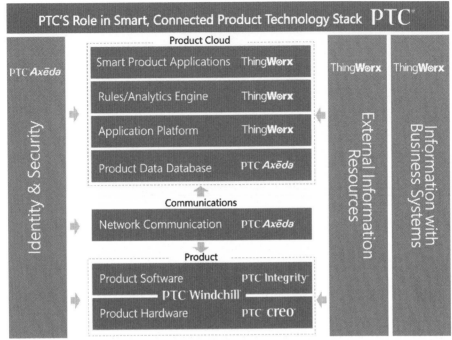

Figure 2.3: PTC IoT Framework

While PTC doesn't manufacture **Things**, its lifecycle product management application, Windchill, and CAD application, Creo, can be used to build next-generation machines. PTC's Axeda provides both cloud-based service and software for **connect**ing products and machines, as well as **collect**ion services. ColdLight, another acquisition, is the basis of PTC's **learn**ing technology. ColdLight's Neuron analyzes data, detects patterns, builds statistically validated predictive models, and sends information to virtually any type of application or technology. Finally, ThingWorx is the middleware that helps build applications to **do** something with the data. ThingWorx has been used to implement predictive maintenance and system-monitoring apps, which PTC says enables significantly faster deployment of applications than conventional technology.

Industry

While GE and PTC represent two large companies making significant investments in software, the industry is considerably larger. Later we'll discuss other suppliers of Things, technology to build Things, and solutions for connecting Things, collecting the data, learning from it and doing something with it. As with any emerging area (like cloud computing) there are both established players and startups. While we cannot cover all of them, you'll hopefully get a sense of who some of the current players are and the potential for the future.

Summary

For the remainder of this book we'll use the Things, Connect, Collect, Learn and Do framework. First, we'll dive into each of the components and discuss fundamental principles and show you how these principles are put into practice. At the end we'll discuss complete solutions implemented by both manufacturers of precision machines as well as those who use them to implement precision agriculture, power, water, healthcare or transportation.

3

Things Principles

Enterprise Things—be it a gene sequencer, locomotive, or water chiller—are becoming both smarter and more connected. In this chapter we'll cover some of the fundamental principles you should be aware of when building the next enterprise Thing. Sensors are beginning to follow Moore's Law by becoming dramatically less expensive each year. They're also becoming increasingly attached to low-cost computers, which can range from simple microcontrollers to fully featured CPUs supporting either the ARM or Intel instruction set architecture. More powerful software can be supported with a move to more powerful processors, so we'll cover some basic operating systems. Finally, we'll discuss a couple security fundamentals that anyone building enterprise Things should consider.

Sensors

While there are hundreds of kinds of sensors, we're going to use those found in smart phones to get more specific. Let's start with one of the most commonly used sensors: the accelerometer. As the name implies, an accelerometer measures the acceleration of the handset relative to free fall. The same sensor is also used to determine a device's orientation along its three axes. Apps use this data to tell if a phone is in portrait or landscape orientation and if its screen is facing upward or downward. The gyroscope is another sensor that can provide orientation information but with greater precision. This particular sensor tells you how much a phone has been rotated and in which direction.

Another sensor is the magnetometer, which measures the strength and direction of the magnetic field and is used in both compass and metal-detection apps.

The proximity sensor works by shining a beam of infrared light that is reflected from the object and picked up by the detector; it is then placed near the earpiece of a phone to let it know that you're probably on a call and that the screen has to be turned off.

Phones also have light sensors to measure the brightness of the ambient light and they use this data to automatically adjust the display's brightness.

Some phones have a built-in barometer, which measures atmospheric pressure and is used to determine its height above sea level, which results in improved GPS accuracy. Every phone has a thermometer, and some have more than one. If a component is detected to be overheating, the system shuts itself down to prevent damage.

Samsung pioneered the use of an air-humidity sensor in its Galaxy phones, data from which was used in an app to tell whether or not the user was in his or her "comfort zone"—one with optimal air temperature and humidity.

A pedometer is a sensor used to count the number of steps the user has taken; some phones just use data from the accelerometer, but a dedicated pedometer is more accurate and power efficient. The Google Nexus 5 is among the few phones that have a true pedometer built in. Some phones, such as the Galaxy X5, have heart-rate monitors. This is implemented by detecting the minute pulsations of the blood vessels inside your finger. And of course, most Apple and Google Pixel users know about fingerprint sensors as a substitute for a lock-screen password.

Finally, a sensor that you wouldn't expect to find is a radiation sensor. The Sharp Pantone 5 features an app to measure the current radiation level in the area. Adding the microphone and the cameras to the list gives us a figure of at least 14 different sensors just on your phone. And as we'll illustrate later, this is just a small number of all the potential sensors.

Computer Architecture

All smart, connected machines contain some kind of central processing unit (CPU) capable of running some software. As Things can be constrained by power consumption, physical size and cost, there are a number of tradeoffs that can be made in the basic architecture of the CPU.

At the most basic level, there are classes of microcontrollers that have simple instruction sets with more limited access to memory storage and generally lower power consumption. An example would be the Arduino, which employs an 8-bit, ATmega series microcontroller manufactured by Amtel. While smaller, cheaper and less functional Things can use microcontrollers, the next step is a fully featured instruction set—at this point either from ARM or Intel.

ARM is a Reduced Instruction Set Computer (RISC) that requires significantly fewer transistors to implement the instruction set than typical Intel x86 processors in most personal computers. As a result, this approach reduces costs, heat and power use. Raspberry Pi is based around a 32-bit ARM processor. The Apple A7, which powers this generation of phones and tablets, is a 64-bit system ARM CPU designed by Apple.

While ARM is in use by many, Intel's x86 architecture still powers lots of servers and laptops, and as a result, has many software development tools. Intel Atom is the brand name for a line of ultra-low-power microprocessors from Intel.

Software

There are many different operating system or run-time environments for executing software on a particular Thing. Decisions here will revolve around the memory footprint the software requires, the development environment and the real-time requirements.

Footprint
In computing, the memory footprint of an executable program indicates its run-time-memory requirements while the program

executes. Larger programs have larger memory footprints. Software programs themselves often do not contribute the largest portions to their own memory footprints; rather, structures introduced by the run-time environment can increase the footprint. In a Java program, the memory footprint is predominantly made up of the Java Virtual Machine (JVM) run-time environment.

Software Development Environment
A software development environment, sometimes called an integrated development environment (IDE), is software that provides comprehensive facilities to computer programmers for software development. A software development environment normally consists of a source-code editor, build automation tools and a debugger. For programming the microcontrollers, the Arduino platform provides an IDE, which includes support for the C, C++ and Java programming languages. As a builder of enterprise Things, you'll have to consider what kind of IDE you'll want for your programmers.

Operating System
An operating system, or run-time environment, contains software that is commonly used by many applications. You're likely familiar with Linux and Microsoft Windows in the world of IoP applications. In IoT applications there can be the need for what is called real-time operating systems.

A real-time operating system (RTOS) is an operating system intended to serve time-critical applications. Processing-time requirements (including any OS delay) are measured in tenths of a second or shorter. A key characteristic of an RTOS is the level of its consistency concerning the amount of time it takes to accept and complete an application's task. Key factors in an RTOS are minimal interrupt latency and minimal thread-switching latency, as it's valued more for how quickly or predictably it can respond rather than for the amount of work it can perform in a given period of time. Wind River is an example company that provides an RTOS commonly used to support the needs for real-time processing. Of course, as processors become faster and the needs of any smart machine become wider, we may end up using conventional operating systems in many cases.

On the other hand, Android, iOS and Windows are built for the Internet of People. As a result, considerable effort has gone into building user interfaces. But why does an operating system for a compressor, boom lift or wind turbine need a user interface? Companies like Atomiton have emerged to build software that makes it simple to add sensors and manage security and updates—software we need for the Internet of Things.

Security

There are many aspects of security relevant in the discussion of IoT. Here we're going to focus on the security and integrity of the software. After all, many more security breaches have happened by compromising the software than in any other area.

Secure Boot
Whenever the machine powers up, the first software to run is termed "the boot." Secure boot secures the overall booting process by preventing the loading of any software that is not signed with an acceptable digital signature. When secure boot is enabled it allows a key to be written to the firmware; once the key is written, secure boot allows only software with the key to be loaded.

No Bad Software

Many of you are familiar with antivirus software on your laptops or PCs; antivirus software is built to detect bad software that could compromise a computer. A famous case was the Stuxnet virus, which ended up taking over the centrifuges of Iran's uranium enrichment plants. Stuxnet specifically targets programmable logic controllers (PLCs), which are used to control machines—in this case centrifuges for separating nuclear material. Stuxnet functions by targeting machines using Microsoft Windows OS and networks, and then seeks out Siemens Step 7 software. Stuxnet reportedly ruined almost one-fifth of Iran's nuclear centrifuges.

All Good Software

A patch is a piece of software designed to update a computer's software. While some patches are designed to improve usability or performance, there are also patches designed to repair security vulnerabilities. Patch management is the process of strategizing and planning which patches should be applied to which systems at a specified time. In IoP applications, companies like VMware, Oracle and Microsoft easily release hundreds of relevant security patches per year.

Standards

You can add compute and connectivity to practically any machine to transfer bits into the internet; however, you also need standards that establish consistent and well-understood protocols for electronic data exchange that can be universally adopted. Standards help with fuel compatibility and interoperability across manufacturers. Standards also simplify product development and decrease time to market. In this section, we'll briefly discuss the ISO 15143-2 standard used for communications from the machine to the internet, and the SAE J1939 standard used for communications within the vehicle.

ISO 15143-2
Specific to the construction industry, electronic data exchange on the construction job site has become a key technology, enabling the IoT evolution from predominately manual processes to more automated data collection and communication.

For this purpose, the ISO 15143-2 standard was developed—partially by the Association of Equipment Manufacturers (AEM) and the Association of Equipment Management Professionals (AEMP)—to support earth-moving and mobile, road-construction machinery. It defines a data schema for the purpose of providing data directly from the equipment manufacturer or provider to the equipment owner in a standardized format for the use and convenience of equipment owners with mixed fleets.

It also defines a set of web services that provide information about fleets of mobile equipment and their associated telematics data. The information about a fleet is provided as a resource, typically on the internet at a known URL (Uniform Resource Location). Any number of fleets can be represented, each with its own URL.

Clients can access these resources by sending HTTPS GET requests to the server at the given location. The server responds with an equipment information document whose vocabulary is defined in the ISO 15143-2 specification.

SAE J1939
The Society of Automotive Engineers (SAE) defined the J1939 standard, which defines the recommended practice to be used for

communication and diagnostics among vehicle components. Originating in the car and heavy-duty truck industry in the United States, it is now widely used in other parts of the world.

SAE J1939 defines five layers in the seven-layer OSI network model, which includes the Controller Area Network (CAN) ISO 11898 specification. Under J1939/11 and J1939/15, the data rate is specified as 250kbps, with J1939/14 specifying 500kbps.

SAE J1939 is used in the commercial vehicle area for communication throughout the vehicle, with the physical layer defined in ISO 11898. A different physical layer is used between the tractor and trailer, specified in ISO 11992.

Of course, standards alone do not make for a revolution. We still need to add compute and connectivity to the machines used in construction so ultimately, the manufacturers, owners and users of the machines can be more productive and safer at the job site.

Packaging

Packaging is a major discipline within the field of electronic engineering and it includes a wide variety of technologies. Packaging must consider protection from mechanical damage, cooling, radio-frequency noise emission and electrostatic discharge. Industrial equipment made in small quantities may use standardized, commercially available enclosures such as card cages or prefabricated boxes. Mass-market consumer devices may have highly specialized packaging to increase consumer appeal.

One of the packaging technologies used in high volume is called system on a chip (SoC). An SoC is an integrated circuit that combines all components of a computer or other electronic system into a single semiconductor chip. It may contain digital, analog, mixed-signal and often radio-frequency functions. The contrast with a microcontroller is one of degree; microcontrollers typically have fewer than 100KB of memory, whereas an SoC is used for more powerful processors capable of running software that needs a larger memory footprint (e.g., Linux). When it's not feasible to construct an SoC for a particular application, an alternative is a system in package (SiP), comprising a number of chips in a single package. In large volumes, an SoC is believed to be more cost effective than an SiP because it increases the yield of the fabrication and its packaging is simpler.

In the next chapter, we'll see a few current examples of enterprise Things.

4

Things in Practice

Today, modern phones can have up to 14 sensors and you can buy a powerful computer for $100. These things help to partially explain why Things used across industries, including construction, are getting smarter and more instrumented.

In this chapter we'll review a range of machines used in construction—as well as the many ways they are being made smarter.

Track Loaders

We start by describing track loaders, as their ability to perform almost every task on a job site makes them part of many companies' fleets. A track loader consists of a tracked (not wheeled) chassis with a loader for digging and loading material.

In the mid-80s, Takeuchi introduced the world's first compact track loader. Today, Takeuchi builds a line of five track loader models, including the Takeuchi TL12V2.

All TL12V2s are equipped with Takeuchi Fleet Management (TFM). At the machine level, TFM is implemented with ZTR Control Systems' (ZTR) telematics hardware that Takeuchi installs in its factory as part of the manufacturing process. Data is gathered from the control units by a connection to the machine's CAN bus, as all onboard sensors feed into it.

TFM-enabled Takeuchi machines provide a range of sensor-based information, including engine torque, injector metering rail pressure, hydraulic oil temperature, machine location, engine speed, battery voltage, engine oil pressure, engine coolant temperature, fuel level, fuel consumption rate, DPF (diesel particulate filter) status, trip meters and last communication. In addition, standard J1939 fault codes, as well as Takeuchi-specific fault codes, are provided.

Boom Lifts

A boom lift is a type of aerial lift that supports a hydraulic arm that is capable of maneuvering around obstacles. There are two basic types of boom lifts: articulating and telescopic. Articulating boom lifts have arms that bend, making it easier to move the bucket around things. Telescopic boom lifts have straight arms. Telescopic lifts usually have higher weight capacities, but they are more difficult to maneuver.

JLG is a leading designer and manufacturer of boom lifts, as well as scissor lifts, telehandlers, stock lifters and utility vehicles. JLG's 40-, 60-, and 80-foot boom lifts make up 60% of the market and are connected with an ORBCOMM PT7000 device, which interfaces to the machine's CAN bus. It includes sensors to measure location, on/off, battery level, duty cycle, load type, engine speed, RPM, fault codes, engine or idol hours, fuel consumption, battery voltage and geo-fencing.

The ORBCOMM PT7000 has four digital inputs, two digital outputs and four analog inputs. It supports both J1939 and J1798 protocols, meaning it can support multiple CAN buses. It's powered by the machine but also has a 9-volt backup battery.

Retrofitting Existing Equipment

Given that construction equipment can exist in fleets for seven years or more, a rental agency or contractor may have machines in their existing fleets that need to be retrofitted to connect to the internet.

United Rentals represents one such example, with over 450,000 pieces of non-connected construction equipment in its fleet that needed to be retrofitted with connect capabilities. Customers were basically saying: If you can get 12-volt power off the machine either by engine or battery, then we want telematics on it.

United Rentals' retrofit strategy involved working with ZTR, who engineered three types of edge solutions:

Temporary

The temporary solution is a portable "Slap Track" device, which is a small and simple M4 unit that attaches to a machine to provide location and an estimate of run hours based on vibrations. This device is deployed predominately for short-term installs. It utilizes a 4G LTE Cat 1 cellular-based radio with a 56-channel GPS receiver. The device is IP-67 and completely self-contained with battery, GPS, and communications in one package, making it easy to install and capable of withstanding harsh work environments.

Retrofit

The retrofit solution is an M6 device that provides basic machine connectivity, giving visibility into run hours, location, battery level, low battery voltage alerts, fuel level and output control. The device utilizes a 4G LTE Cat 1 cellular radio with a 3G HSPA fallback. GPS is provided by a 56-channel GPS receiver and internal antennas for both GPS and cellular needs.

The M6 was built to adapt to various retrofit applications so it can be mounted in various locations, is IP-66 rated and is powered by 12-volt and 24-volt battery systems. With internal antennas and a harness with connector solution, the M6 is an easy to install, supportable solution.

New OEM Advanced Monitoring

For new installs, ZTR provides the M8LZT, which delivers advanced connectivity and monitoring that integrates into the equipment's CAN bus J1939 network to provide run hours, location, engine data, machine faults, emissions data, regeneration status, fuel level and other machine sensor data. The M8LZT comes with optional 4G LTE Cat 1 or 3G/2G variants that can be used for worldwide deployments, along with a 56-channel GPS receiver. The M8LZT also comes with

BLE Bluetooth® connectivity, providing opportunities to connect and collect data from Bluetooth® devices and sensors.

Engines

With power output ranging from 110 to 163hp, the four-cylinder Cummins QSB4.5 T4 (Tier 4) engine delivers performance comparable to some six-cylinder engines, without the excess bulk and weight. *Tier 4* refers to a set of emissions requirements established by the Environmental Protection Agency (EPA) to reduce emissions of particulate matter, oxides of nitrogen, and other harmful toxins from new, non-road diesel engines.

This engine's fuel system not only controls and reduces particulate matter, but also helps deliver quicker throttle response, while a more efficient variable-flow turbocharger optimizes boost. Furthermore, the Electronic Control Module (ECM) enables multiple injection events per combustion cycle, which increases the power output while reducing noise.

The increase in power requires improved air handling, which is made possible by the Cummins Direct Flow air filter. This filter utilizes an innovative "V-block" rectangular configuration that eliminates the wasted space in round air filter elements. Also available is an optional pre-cleaner cover that removes 95% of particles before they reach the filter, which is especially helpful on dusty job sites.

The QSB4.5 engine has 52 different sensors for engine protection, monitoring and control, including sensors for air handling, fuel system, after treatment, and basic engine monitoring of coolant temperature, intake temperature and pressure, coolant level, oil pressure and more. Inside the construction machine there are between 1,500 and 3,000 messages per second being reported on the CAN bus.

Depending on the machine, these messages fall into two broad categories: public and private. Regulatory bodies require that public messages be reported and can vary from on-highway to off-highway to marine applications. Cummins, however, is particularly interested in private messages. All of the data today is event data, but in the future, there will be time-series, sensor data as well.

Diesel Generators

Diesel generators are used for onsite and backup power. One such generator is the instrumented Engel Inverter Diesel Generator. There are several types of data available from this generator, including cellular signal percentage, engine coolant temperature, engine oil pressure, fuel level, last communication, last data collection time, low coolant temperature and more.

Environmental Monitors

Many job sites are environmentally sensitive, meaning there are requirements governing that vibration, noise and airborne particulates be kept to a minimum during certain periods of time. For example, a construction project may be located next to a hospital's neonatal care unit, in which case the contractor has to ensure that there is no jack hammering or other noisy activities that will disturb the doctors, nurses or patients at the hospital.

Historically, environmental monitoring has been a low-tech, manual process that includes mounted sensors, red light bulbs, and an hourly, in-person check of each monitoring station to look at sensor readings and to update the numbers on a paper log sheet. This approach has many obvious limitations, not the least of which is the inability to communicate in real time with the contractor or the customer if there are issues at the job site, such as noise levels being above acceptable levels.

Skanska is a multinational construction company based in Stockholm, Sweden and is the fifth largest construction company in the world. Notable Skanska projects include London's 30 St Mary Ax building (commonly known as "The Gherkin"), the University Medical Center in New Orleans, the World Trade Center Transportation Hub, and the Meadowland Sports Complex (home to the NFL's New York Jets and Giants and the 2014 Super Bowl).

Working with Microsoft, Skanska designed its own environmental monitor called the inSite Monitor. It allows a construction team to monitor a range of environmental conditions, replacing pencil and paper with a network-connected device that has the ability to provide real-time notifications about environmental issues at the job site.

The inSite Monitor includes sensors that measure temperature, humidity, water leakage, atmospheric pressure, noise, vibration and air particulates.

It uses a custom-built board running Qualcomm's DragonBoard 410c processor. On the software side it runs the Windows 10 IoT Core operating system, which is a very small footprint version of the Windows, targeted for small-form-factor devices.

Robotics

Some jobs at the construction site require a degree of repetitive action. Bricklaying is one such example, especially when the wall to be built is long, straight and flat.

The SAM100 was the first commercially available, semi-automated bricklaying robot for onsite masonry construction. SAM is a collaborative robot designed to work with the help of trained masons, relying on one mason to operate it, a tender to load it with bricks and mortar, and another mason to secure wall ties, remove excess mortar and lay bricks in corners or other challenging areas.

SAM's basic components include a large robotic arm with multiple joints, a laser eye that detects depths and distances required to place each brick, a pair of story poles at the left and right of the work area, a CAM (computer-aided manufacturing)-generated design for mapping the job and a tablet-based control panel.

SAM includes several sensors that measure and track velocity, incline angles, orientation, outside and enclosure temperature, humidity, run hours, GPS, safety and more. For instance, SAM measures the slump and quality of mortar being applied. All data generated is time stamped to the millisecond. Before starting work on a wall, masons first use digital maps of the architectural blueprint to take measurements of the work area before programming SAM accordingly.

In an eight-hour day, a typical mason will lay between 350 to 550 bricks, whereas SAM lays 350 bricks per *hour*, never needing to stop for a coffee or bathroom break.

Augmented Reality Glasses

Before a building or space can be signed over as *code compliant*, it has to be inspected by a building inspector—someone with a well-trained eye to notice discrepancies and code violations. The traditional inspection routine includes a walkthrough with clipboard in hand, writing down code violations and other issues, such as improper window sealings or an exposed area of the fire control system. The building inspector also completes a code inspection sheet in the form of a paper punch list. After the walkthrough, the inspector manually types up his notes or transfers them onto more paper, depending on which municipality the building is in.

This process is not only extremely mundane for the inspector, but also error prone, as handwriting may be illegible, the inspector may not recall exactly where he pinpointed a particular discrepancy, or there may be a miscommunication with the contractor. It's not an uncommon scenario for inspector-noted discrepancies to either get missed or to have something corrected that didn't need to be. This wastes time and money, as unresolved problems still need to be addressed, requiring workers to return to the job to fix the unresolved issues.

Another challenge occurs with 3D building information models (BIMs). Each stage of the construction process—such as mechanical, plumbing, electrical and HVAC—has its own model, but as there is no model-design standard, conflicts can exist when the models are combined and applied. For example, a plumber might find that he can't do his work because the electrician placed wiring where the pipes are supposed to go. Addressing this challenge today involves another manual process called *clash detection* where someone takes model segments and clashes them together in a 3D environment in an attempt to inspect and find modeling issues before building begins.

To help resolve these challenges, augmented reality (AR) glasses are being deployed in construction projects. AR glasses can overlay and present the BIM, at scale, into the wearer's field of view so he or she can see what the model says should be there versus what is actually there.

DAQRI is one such vendor whose Smart Glasses™ are being applied on job sites. DAQRI Smart Glasses™ have two components. First, the headband includes the optics and sensor packages, plus a secondary processor dedicated to the computer-vision function. The second component is a compute pack that contains the main processor, memory, storage and battery. The headband weighs 335g, while the compute pack weighs 496g. Both components also have built-in, rechargeable, 5800mAh lithium ion batteries, each of which lasts about 4–6 hours with normal use.

The compute pack contains the computational capability of a high-end gaming laptop, using a 6th Generation 3Ghz Intel® Core™ m7 Processor with 8GB RAM and 64GB SSD. DAQRI uses a proprietary Visual Operating System™ and a dedicated vision-processing unit that enables movement in six degrees of freedom. In other words, where it is moving along the X, Y and Z axes and where it is rotating between X, Y and Z coordinates (pitch, yaw and roll).

The headband includes a number of cameras and sensors. Depth sensors provide information for environmental reconstruction while other sensors track temperature, humidity, noise and location. To perform the augmented reality function, the computer overlays the

BIM with what the camera sees, what the sensors pick up, where the glasses are in the physical world, and if the glasses are moving.

For a number of reasons, the AR glasses don't include GPS. First, they are designed to run in GPS-denied environments. Next, GPS accuracy is only guaranteed to a few meters, which is not good enough to provide content in augmented reality. It makes a huge difference if the layered information is a few meters off the rendering of the physical space in front of the user. The level of accuracy of the DAQRI devices depends on the task requested of the device, but in general the level of precision is within approximately one centimeter. This accuracy capability is solved by the on-board, computer-vision-based tracking, which is a proprietary DAQRI technology.

Next

Our devices and machines—our Things—are set to become much smarter. Today you can equip a 1GHz ARM architecture processor with 512MB of memory and 2GB of flash memory storage for less than $100; this computer is slightly larger than a couple of coins. Furthermore, you'll have WiFi and Bluetooth® connectivity and support for a full Linux distribution included. This computer can connect to 128 sensors, which brings us to the rapid decrease in the cost of sensors. Before long, sensors that cost $10 today will only cost $1. An accelerometer today is already less than $3. Of course, the last time we ended up with millions of smart Things it was called a PC and Intel dominated on the hardware side and Microsoft dominated on the software side. Will it be the same this time around?

One thing that does not need to be the same is our approach to securing these Things. It's always been a game of catch-up, as most of the Things we built for people didn't predict the danger of connecting to global networks. Perhaps this time around, we'll engineer our machines to be able to protect themselves.

5

Connect Principles

Connecting Things requires a diverse set of technologies based on the amount of data that needs to be transmitted, how far it needs to go and how much power you have. Furthermore, you have many choices at a higher level on how to manage, protect and secure the connection. Here we'll provide a brief tutorial on connecting machines and some of the fundamental principles. If you work in networking, just skip ahead.

Networking Fundamentals

In networking you'll eventually hear about the Open Systems Interconnection (OSI) stack, which is a conceptual model that characterizes and standardizes the communication functions of a telecommunication or computing system without regard to their underlying internal structure and technology. Its goal is the interoperability of diverse communication systems with standard protocols. The model partitions a communication system into abstraction layers; the original version of the model defined seven layers.

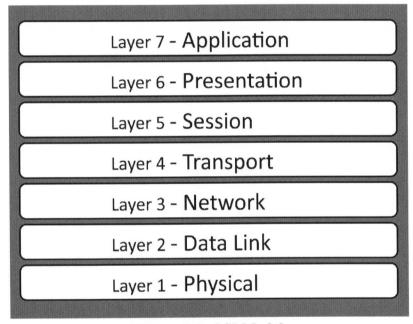

Figure 5.1: OSI Model

A layer serves the layer above it and is served by the layer below it. For example, a layer that provides error-free communications across a network provides the path needed by applications above it, while it calls the next lower layer to send and receive packets that comprise the contents of that path. This stack is a useful framework to understand the different levels of connectivity from a purely electric level all the way to the application level. In this chapter we'll focus on the data-link layer and the higher-level, application layer.

Data-Link Layer

The data-link layer provides node-to-node data transfer, which is a link between two directly connected nodes. It detects and possibly corrects errors that may occur in the physical layer. It defines the protocol to establish and terminate a connection between two physically connected devices and defines the protocol for flow control between them. The data-link layer is responsible for controlling how devices in a network gain access to data and permission to transmit it. It is also responsible for identifying and encapsulating network layer protocols, and controls error checking and packet synchronization. Connection technology including Ethernet, WiFi and Zigbee all operate at the data-link layer.

Range vs. Power

In cases where the Thing cannot be physically connected to the internet—either because of location or the fact that it's mobile—you will need some form of wireless technology. There are numerous choices: WiFi, 3G, 4G, Zigbee, NFC, LoRaWAN, satellite, etc. Which strategy or strategies you choose depends on a couple of fundamental principles related to power consumption, range requirements, data rates, costs, size of antenna and the environment.

	WiFi	ZigBee	Bluetooth	NFC
POWER	High	Low	Classic: Mid LE/Smart: Low	Tag: Zero Reader: Very Low
RANGE	30-100 m	10-20 m	10 m	<0.1 m

Figure 5.2: Range vs. Power

Fig. 5.2 shows the tradeoff between range and power consumption for four different connection technologies. WiFi, which has a range of 30–100 meters, requires considerably more power than Bluetooth®, which has a maximum range of 10 meters, or NFC, where the range is less than 0.1 meters.

As a rule, a wireless signal attenuates with the square of distance, which means that doubling your range requires a four-fold increase in power—a bigger battery.

Some applications may be able to operate within a closed, proprietary wireless network. As an example, McCrometer's water sensors use the band from 560–480MHz, which has been allocated for this type of communication. A farm or water district can purchase a license for a portion of this spectrum from the FCC that's good for 10 years and covers a radius of 20 miles. At this frequency, UHF (ultra high frequency) is capable of reaching 1–12 miles, depending on the terrain.

Range vs. Data Rate

Another tradeoff is range versus speed. As frequency rises, available bandwidth typically rises, but distance and ability to overcome obstacles is reduced. For any given distance, a 2.4GHz installation will have roughly 8.5dB of additional path loss (3dB is a 50% loss) when compared to 900MHz.

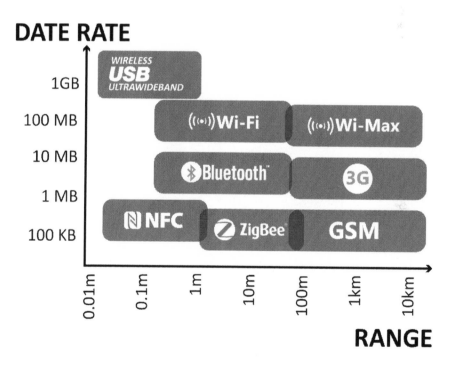

Figure 5.3: Range vs. Data Rate

So, higher frequencies have higher bandwidth capability, but require more power to achieve the same range. Lower frequencies have lower bandwidth, but can achieve longer distance; however, lower frequencies unfortunately require larger antennas to achieve the same gain.

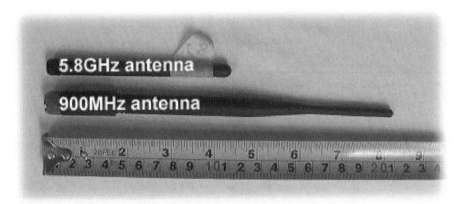

Figure 5.4: Size of Antenna

Environment also plays a role in network performance, as anyone watching satellite TV on a rainy day surely knows. Manufacturers advertise *line of sight* range figures. Line of sight means that from antenna-A you can see antenna-B; being able to see the building that antenna B is in doesn't count. For every obstacle in the path, de-rate the line of sight figure specified for each. The type, location and number of obstacles all play a role in path loss.

Application Layer

Perhaps one of the largest areas of competition in the IoT space is at the application layer, and in making it easy to connect new machines and pull data into a variety of collection architectures, which we'll discuss in the next chapter. Whether you're building a coffee pot or a generator, you're faced with a number of implementation decisions. Some have counted more than 100 suppliers. With such a large number of end applications to target, and such broad technology and data needs in terms of the platform, the number of players is not surprising. Some of the newer players include companies like Arrayent, Ayla Networks and Electric Imp. These companies have focused on low-cost and consumer machines including water heaters, postage stamp meters, washing machines, garage-door openers and medical wearables.

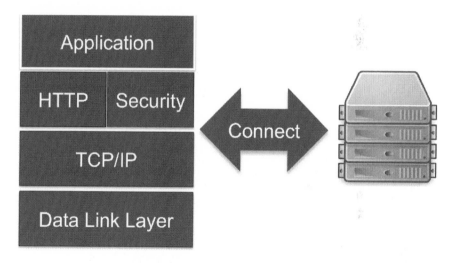

Figure 5.5: Application Layer

Some companies have been more focused on vertical markets, like Silver Spring Networks in the power industry. Silver Spring provides Zigbee radio technology, as well as higher-level connection protocols. Smaller players like Axeda and 2lemetry have been acquired by larger players—PTC and Amazon—and made part of a larger IoT framework.

Furthermore, there have been more traditional suppliers like Appareo, which supplies technology to AGCO. Appareo also makes its connection solutions backward compatible to support older farm equipment with the added ability to deal with harsher environments than those found in the home environment. Some of these companies will also package cellular plans as part of the complete solution. A good example is ZTR, which got its start in train control.

Network Security

Network security starts with authentication, commonly with a username and password, which is called *one-factor* authentication. But with increased attention to security, many are implementing *two-factor* authentication, which requires the use of something the person physically owns. This could be a special-purpose device or, as many of you have seen, a cell phone that receives codes from the application to verify your identity a second time.

Once authenticated, firewalls enforce access policies such as what services are accessible by the network users. A firewall monitors and controls the incoming and outgoing network traffic based on a set of security rules; they typically establish a barrier between a trusted, secure internal network and another outside network, such as the internet, that is assumed to be unsecure or untrusted.

Increasingly, firewalls also check for potentially harmful content such as computer worms or Trojans being transmitted over the network. Anti-virus software or intrusion prevention systems help detect and inhibit the action of such bad software. Network traffic may also be logged for audit purposes and later high-level analysis.

Finally, at the connection level, encryption is used to protect the transmitted data, as there is no way to physically secure the connection and prevent an attacker from being able to see the transmission. Encryption relies on a set of keys shared between the transmitter and the receiver. It also assumes that brute force attacks of trying every key will not be successful without massive computer resources. While encrypting transmissions can provide additional security, access control of the keys now becomes equally important.

As threats increase and Things are increasingly networked and thereby accessible, the demand for innovation only increases. At this point, most of the technology developed has been for the Internet of People. But Things are not People, so why would an Integrated Access Management (IAM) application built for the Internet of People work for the Internet of Things? Companies like Uniquid are building IAM for IoT, where no one will expect a tractor, gene sequencer or forklift to change its password every 90 days (making sure to add a special character) or answer security questions. Besides, what would a blood analyzer choose as its favorite sport?

6

Connect in Practice

Across industries and use cases, connecting Things generally requires a diverse set of technologies based on the amount of data that needs to be transmitted, how far it needs to go, how much power you have to consume and how big the antenna is. In this chapter we'll focus on the wide variety of connection technologies implemented to connect construction machines.

Cellular Network

If you're working on a job site, the predominately available network is cellular. For example, machines managed through United Rentals' Total Control® fleet management system connect primarily via a 3G cellular network for data transfer.

Likewise, Takeuchi track loaders connect across a 3G cellular network operating over GSM 850, 900, 1800 and 1900 MHz frequency bands. The wireless carrier provides a private VPN so all data is protected during transmission. Location is provided over satellite through a 56-channel GPS using a Satellite-based Augmentation System (SBAS).

If you're looking for a secure and reliable mobile connection between your Things and most of the countries in the world, Vodafone can provide that network. They achieve this by combining their mobile operations in 26 countries with partnerships in 55 others, in addition to having fixed broadband operations in 17 markets. They leverage these multiple network connections to ensure a much higher degree of availability and performance by providing multiple-path routing so that even a pacemaker can have a guaranteed level of connection service around the world.

Vodafone leverages a global footprint augmented by strategic operator relationships outside of the operating companies, which is further augmented by more than 600 roaming partnerships. Vodafone uniquely combines this massive footprint with a global SIM providing a single means (e.g., a SKU) for products to be distributed worldwide.

Furthermore, a single global support system provides a one-stop solution. This is all managed by a dedicated global M2M platform called GDSP or Global Data Services Platform.

WiFi

Most of you are familiar with WiFi technology, which has been the preferred mechanism to connect people to the internet from offices to Starbucks. WiFi can reach up to 100 feet and can support hundreds of Megabits per second. Compared to Zigbee and Bluetooth®, WiFi consumes a lot of power, but that said, it is used extensively in office settings.

The inSite Monitor developed by Skanska for environmental monitoring acts as an IoT field gateway connecting sensor data to processes running on the Microsoft Azure Cloud. Network connectivity to the internet is handled via WiFi, but there are also two USB ports for connecting to a MiFi network if desired.

Cisco, a leader in networking, offers the Cisco 819 Integrated Services Router, which is the smallest Cisco IOS software router with support for integrated wireless WAN and wireless LAN capabilities. The Cisco 819 also has a virtual machine capability that can support the execution of software developed by third parties.

With the Cisco 819 router, data is transferred via a secure, Transport Layer Security (TLS) connection. TLS and its predecessor, Secure Sockets Layer (SSL)—both of which are frequently referred to as SSL—are cryptographic protocols designed to provide communications security over a network. Several versions of the protocols are in widespread use in applications such as web browsing, email, internet faxing, instant messaging and voice over IP (VoIP). Major websites including Google, YouTube and Facebook use TLS to secure all communications between their servers and web browsers.

Satellite

It is not that uncommon for construction sites to exist outside of cellular coverage, which is particularly true in rural areas around the world. As a result, satellite transmission remains one way to talk to the machine.

In fact, many machines are equipped with a number of networking options. For instance, JLG scissor and boom lifts connect using 3G cellular, Bluetooth® or WiFi, but can also connect via satellite for use in remote areas or mines.

An example outside of construction is locomotives, which can often be without WiFi or cellular connectivity. In response, GE manufactures the LOCOCOMM, a Communications Management Unit (CMU) applicable to both GE and non-GE locomotives. It uses an Intel single-board computer with 256MB of memory and up to 4GB of flash storage running on a Microsoft Windows NT operating system. The system operates with no external cooling and is powered directly by a 74-volt locomotive battery.

In addition to communications, the CMU contains an integrated GPS that provides a Differential Global Positioning System—an enhancement to GPS that provides improved location accuracy from the 15-meter nominal accuracy to about 10 centimeters in the best implementations. The unit uses satellite for small amounts of time-sensitive data and larger files are transferred over WiFi when the train reaches its destination.

Zigbee

Zigbee is an IEEE 802.15.4-based specification for a suite of high-level communication protocols used to create personal area networks with small, low-power digital radios. The technology is intended to be simpler and less expensive than Bluetooth® or WiFi. Its low-power consumption limits transmission distances to a line of sight of 10–100 meters.

Zigbee is typically used in low-data-rate applications that require long battery life and secure networking; 128-bit symmetric encryption keys secure the networks. Zigbee has a defined rate of 250kbps.

In the early 2000s, well before machine equipment was routinely updated to include connectivity, a Precision Contractor had the foresight to build a custom hardware and software system to provide data from the construction machines used in the field. At that time, the cost of a cellular connection was $30–$50 per month, so connecting 800 machines was very expensive. As a result, the hub of the network used at this company's construction sites is the fuel-control panel, which is connected to the company's servers by WiFi or cellular. All of the construction machines are then Zigbee connected to the fuel-control panels. Today, about 50 fuel trucks support around 800 connected machines.

LoRaWAN

Traditionally, wireless solutions could only rely on a few different technologies for communication. They could accept the limited range of standards-based, local-area technologies (e.g., WiFi, Zigbee and

Bluetooth®), or pay the costs for wide-area cellular technology. A new market is now emerging with the deployment of low-power wide-area networks (LPWAN). These technologies hope to bridge the gap between current LAN and WAN technologies to allow for low-cost machine connections.

LPWAN specification is designed for wireless, battery-powered Things. The network architecture is typically laid out in a star-of-stars topology in which gateways relay messages between end devices and a central network server in the backend. Gateways are connected to the network server via standard IP connections while end devices use single-hop wireless communication to one or many gateways. All end-point communication is generally bi-directional but also supports operations such as multicast, enabling software upgrades over the air or other mass distribution messages to reduce the on-air communication time.

Communication between end devices and gateways is spread out on different frequency channels and data rates. The selection of the data rate is a tradeoff between range and message duration. Due to the technology, communications with different data rates do not interfere with each other and create a set of virtual channels increasing the capacity of the gateway.

LoRaWAN data rates range from 0.3kbps to 50kbps. LoRaWAN's use of lower frequency (sub-GHz) bands means the signals can penetrate the core of large structures and subsurface deployments within a range of 2km.

Tata Communications (Tata) has announced plans for an India-wide LoRaWAN network following successful trials in Mumbai and Delhi, joining several other major telcos in adopting the technology. Orange has plans for a France-wide network and Telstra has begun early trials in Melbourne, Australia. LoRaWAN-technology pioneer Semtech Corporation has been selected by Tata to deploy the network with full coverage planned for Mumbai, Delhi and Bangalore.

Firewalls

For this example, we borrow from the oil and gas industry. Because oil and gas platforms are within line of site of land, most of the traditional communication has been via microwave; however, modern, bigger platforms are all connected by fiber optic cable. On the platform itself, the network interconnects a large quantity of programmable logic controllers (PLCs), instrumentation, smart, automated equipment and packaged, process-control equipment. In addition, the platform communicates with subsea systems and virtual flow meters using the classic OPC (open platform communications) protocol.

Consequently, there is the potential for large amounts of network traffic and crosstalk. Some of the automation controllers deployed on the platform use a UDP broadcast/multicast protocol, which can further increase the volume of network traffic. Because many automation and control devices cannot filter out extraneous network messages, it can be necessary to protect those devices from excessive traffic.

A platform typically involves a myriad of contractors working on inter-related systems. At some point, the network can be exposed to computer viruses, which have been known to come from infected USB drives from an unwitting contractor.

To protect the facility, some platforms implement an architecture that isolates layers of the business and process control network. The automation and business networks can be isolated using managed switches and logical network segregation. Demilitarized zones may be used to protect the process control system from the internet and the business network.

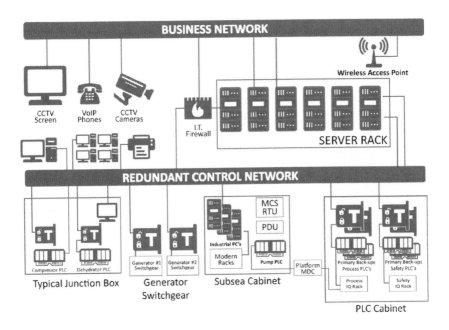

Figure 6.1: Connection Security

Fig. 6.1 shows a deployment on one oil and gas platform. Belden's Tofino security appliance was installed in front of redundant Allen-Bradley ControlLogix PLCs. The security appliances were configured and tested to ensure that the failover of the primary PLC processor to the backup processer would not impact control communications. In turn, the security appliances needed to maintain their security functionality regardless of the switchover state of the PLCs.

Next

Almost all of our communications hardware and software was built to connect people to the internet, but Things are not people; Things can tell you more than people and can talk constantly. We have developed streaming technology to transmit large amounts of information (e.g., movies, games) from servers to people. Our next challenge will be to develop reverse-streaming technology from Things back to the server. As we can control the rate of data transmission, there is the potential to make these reverse-streaming networks efficient. As with streaming, we can afford to drop a few bits, but what will the network topology and control be like when 100,000 machines want to talk every minute? Some argue we should put more "intelligence" into the machines and send less data. But if we have a low-cost way to collect the data and are able to learn from our Things, why not send the data?

Finally, rather than making security an afterthought (as it has been for IoP applications), we have the potential to engineer protected networks out of the gate to communicate with these Things. Being able to authenticate machines, control access, audit, and protect the information as it flows is going to be important. With Things, it's likely that we'll need to be able to segregate *machine* data (i.e., data that describes the state of the machine such as its fuel-consumption rate or diesel particulate filter status) from *nomic* data (i.e., data that describes what the machine is measuring, such as external temperature, noise and vibration levels). Knowing the state of the machine (machine data) will have different rules than knowing what the individual machines measured (nomic data). This brings us to the next step in the stack: collection.

7

Collect Principles

Things aren't people. One of the ways that's true is that the sheer volume of data that Things can generate is much greater than that of IoP applications. Here we'll cover some fundamental ways that Thing data might be collected and stored, including SQL, NoSQL and time-series collection architectures. And while we all might hope that all data of interest is stored in one way, the reality is that we live in a heterogeneous world. As a result, some technologies have evolved to process data from multiple SQL databases, for both structured and unstructured data. Finally, while much of today's data is collected in on-premises servers, cloud computing offers both a lower cost and higher quality alternative.

SQL RDBMS

SQL, which stands for Structured Query Language, is a special-purpose programming language designed for managing data in a relational database management system (RDBMS). Just like Excel tables, relational database tables consist of columns and rows. Each column contains a different type of attribute and each row corresponds to a single record. The structure of the database is often referred to as the schema.

Databases are much more powerful than spreadsheets in the way data can be manipulated. For example, with databases you can:

- Retrieve all records that match certain criteria
- Update records in bulk
- Cross reference records in different tables

There are many implementations of an RDBMS. For instance, to improve performance by leveraging the decreasing cost of memory, engineering efforts have gone into building in-memory databases (versus running on disk storage).

On the other hand, databases that run on disk storage can often experience improved performance by running in large memory caches, which again use the idea that memory access times are significantly faster than disk-access times.

In response, companies like SanDisk have pioneered the use of flash memory to eliminate the need for rotational disk storage. If you've purchased a MacBook Air in the past few years you might have noticed that the entire disk storage is solid state, meaning the old spinning disk is nowhere to be found. Managing hierarchies of storage based on performance and cost has occupied the industry for years and shows no sign of changing.

Finally, SQL databases are often characterized by the implementation of ACID properties. ACID stands for Atomicity, Consistency, Isolation and Durability. These are a series of properties born to serve the needs of transaction-processing applications.

One of the best use cases of ACID properties is debit-credit. For example, let's say that in a transaction-processing application you debit one account $1,000 and credit the other account $1,000. In this case, the bank wants to make sure that in the event of a failure during the transaction (e.g., software, operator or hardware failure), the results stored in the database are in a consistent state. In other words, a failure doesn't result in zero dollars in both accounts. This feature of SQL is used extensively in almost all IoP applications.

NoSQL

A NoSQL (originally referring to "non-SQL" or "non-relational") database provides a mechanism for storage and retrieval of data that is modeled in means other than the tabular relations used in relational databases. Motivations for this approach include schemaless, simple design and simpler horizontal scaling to clusters of machines. The data structures used by NoSQL databases (e.g., key value, graph or document) differ slightly from those used by default in relational databases, making some operations faster in NoSQL and others faster in relational databases.

Most NoSQL databases lack ACID transactions. Instead they offer a concept of *eventual consistency*, in which database changes are eventually propagated to all nodes (typically within milliseconds) so queries for data might not return updated data immediately.

SQL is better in applications where logical, related or discrete data requirements can be identified up front, where data integrity is essential, and where there is standards-based, proven technology with wide developer experience.

NoSQL is better in applications where there are unrelated, indeterminate or evolving data requirements, simpler or looser project objectives that enable coding efforts to start immediately, and where speed and scalability are imperative.

Time Series

Let's now move to thinking more specifically about collecting data from machines. Machines can deliver data once per hour, minute, second or many times per second. That data could be voltage levels from a generator, CO_2 level from a gas sensor or the number of revolutions per second of a wind turbine.

The fundamental challenge in using a SQL RDBMS for time-series data is how to treat each sample from the time-series within the database. Is a unique sample a unique row in a table with columns of time-stamps and sensor values? If you only had 1,000 machines, each with ten sensors sampling at 20 times per second, that would generate more than 17 billion rows per day. If you were a disk-storage company you'd be happy, but most users would be concerned with the cost and performance implications.

As a result, a number of companies have built time-series databases, sometimes referred to as *historians*. These products include PI from OSIsoft, Proficy Historian from GE, IP21 from AspenTech and eDNA and Wonderware from Schneider Electric.

A real-time historian is like a flight recorder for process data. Rather than relational, it is a temporal database that stores its records in a flat file consisting of simply the name, value, quality and timestamp for a data point. The historian is designed for speed of storage and retrieval of data and can typically process millions of events per second. Most of these databases have designed some type of data compression to reduce the cost of archiving large amounts of time-series data.

As you can guess, there are debates between the SQL RDBMS groups and the time-series folks. Time-series advocates will declare they are able to compress time-series data by a factor of 5,000 versus traditional RDBMS implementations. On the other hand, those who advocate RDBMS solutions declare that there are far more programmers and support, and disk storage is becoming less expensive.

As with traditional RDBMS technology, the open-source community is bringing many other technologies into focus. Some IoT companies, including Ayla Networks and Arrayent, are using Cassandra, which was developed by Facebook to store time-series data. OpenTSDB is another open-source effort in the area.

Heterogeneous Data

Hadoop
Hadoop is a software technology designed for storing and processing large volumes of data distributed across a cluster of commodity servers and commodity storage. In the early 2000s, Google published papers outlining its approach and design principles for handling large volumes of data as it indexed the web. These papers heavily influenced the development of Hadoop. Three of those fundamental design principles are:

- First, given hundreds or even thousands of storage machines, failures are the norm rather than the exception; therefore, constant monitoring, error detection, fault tolerance and automatic recovery must be integral to the system.

- Second, files are huge by traditional standards. Multi-GB files and billions of objects are common. As a result, design assumptions and parameters such as I/O operation and block sizes have to be revisited.

- Third, most files are updated by appending new data rather than overwriting existing data. Random writes within a file are practically non-existent. Once written, the files are read-only and often only read sequentially. Given this access pattern on very large files, appending becomes the focus of performance optimization and atomicity guarantees.

Initially, Hadoop consisted of a distributed file system called HDFS and a data processing and execution model called MapReduce. HDFS stores data on commodity machines, providing high-aggregate bandwidth across the cluster. MapReduce allows the programmer to create parallel programs to process the data.

In addition to these base modules, the term *Hadoop* has evolved to also include a host of tools that can be installed on top of or alongside Hadoop to simplify access and processing of data. These include: HBase, a NoSQL, distributed database modeled after Google's BigTable; Hive, a data-warehouse infrastructure providing SQL-like access to data; Pig, a scripting language for accessing and transforming data; Mahout, a machine-learning library and Spark, an in-memory, cluster-computing framework used for fast-batch processing, event streaming and interactive queries. Some think of Spark as a potential successor to MapReduce.

Splunk

Splunk came from a very different problem space than indexing and searching the web, which drove much of the early work on Hadoop. It was instead designed for system administrators to analyze log files generated by a system's hardware or software.

While a database requires you to define tables and fields before you can store data, Splunk accepts almost anything because it does not have a fixed schema. Instead, it performs field extraction at search time, an approach that allows for greater flexibility. Just as Google crawls any web page without knowing anything about a site's layout, Splunk indexes any kind of machine data that can be represented as text.

During the indexing phase, when Splunk processes incoming data and prepares it for storage, the indexer makes one significant modification: it chops the stream of characters into individual events. Events typically correspond to lines in the log file being processed.

Each event gets a timestamp, typically pulled directly from the input line, and a few other default properties like the originating machine. Then, event keywords are added to an index file to speed up later searches. Splunk stores data directly in the file system, which is great from a scalability and reliability point of view.

Although you can just use simple search terms like a username to see how often that turns up in a given time period, Splunk's Search Processing Language (SPL) allows you to do more. For example, you might want to know which applications are the slowest to start up, making the end user wait the longest. By using a combination of SPL and Unix-like pipe commands, you can discover the answer.

Splunk can run on HDFS with a product they call Hunk. Also, as you can guess, there are now some open-source alternatives including Graylog, which is written in Java and uses a few open-source technologies, including Elasticsearch (a distributed, multitenant-capable, full-text search engine), MongoDB (a NoSQL, cross-platform, document-oriented database) and Apache Kafka (a messaging broker system that allows streamed data to be partitioned across a cluster of machines and has many big-data analysis applications).

Cloud Computing

Much of the data collected today continues to be the traditional, on-premises model that's custom managed by a team of people; the advent of cloud computing promises to both reduce cost but also increase the overall quality of service. Several years ago, Amazon CEO, Jeff Bezos, announced the availability of compute and storage cloud services called EC2 and S3. In 2015, Amazon announced it had reached over $6 billion in revenue. Cloud computing is first and foremost a business model based on a new economic model and driven by technology.

The predominate cost of compute and storage is not the cost of the boxes or even the racks they fit in; instead, it's the cost of managing the security, availability, performance and change of the compute and storage environment. As a simple example, any secure compute and storage infrastructure needs to make sure that every applicable vendor security patch is applied. Being aware of those patches, testing them, and applying them to the environment requires human labor.

Conservatively, the cost to manage infrastructure is at least four times the purchase price per year. In four years, you're spending 16 times the purchase price to manage the boxes—so the cost of the boxes is a relatively small percentage of the overall costs.

To address this high cost of managing infrastructure, cloud service providers can dedicate engineering resources to automate the key processes to manage the security, availability and performance of the compute and storage environments. Through automation, they can both dramatically reduce the cost while also increasing the overall quality of service.

Automation is key because the biggest single source of failure in operational systems is human error. Therefore, as cloud-based infrastructure becomes more complex, people with spreadsheets won't be able to manage it. For example, Silicon Valley startup YotaScale has a customer hosted at AWS with more than 1,235,000 possible infrastructure configurations to choose from for its applications, so trying to find the optimal configuration manually is quite a task.

But the good news is that cloud infrastructures produce a lot of data. One of YotaScale's customers produces over 1GB per day of billing information alone. And the underlying infrastructure for only five of YotaScale's customers collectively produces over 1TB of data per day. To leverage this data and help customers better manage their cloud infrastructure, YotaScale has built an artificial-intelligence-powered infrastructure management application that uses this information to assist IT in describing its current cloud environment, diagnosing issues, and ultimately predicting changes that would help optimize or maintain performance, availability and cost.

Let's now look at a few of these collections implemented in IoT applications across a few industries.

8

Collect in Practice

Once machines, assets or devices are connected, there are a variety of ways the data can be collected. In *Collect Principles* we outlined SQL, NoSQL and time-series databases as some of the fundamental technologies used today. While it would be ideal to have just one database of record, in practice this is never the case. As a result, a variety of technologies, including Hadoop and Splunk, have emerged to process data from multiple sources. In this chapter, we'll take some of the collection principles and see how they're applied in practice in various construction use cases.

United Rentals

United Rentals is one of the largest rental companies in the world. As a renter of equipment, the company focuses on driving operational efficiency and excellence in equipment delivery. Like a systems integrator, United Rentals pulls together multiple platforms and manufacturing tools and prepares them for delivery to its customers in a ready state. This means making sure equipment is fueled, cleaned, operational, charged and delivered on time.

One of United Rentals' main objectives is to help customers save money by more effectively managing rental consumption; in other words, renting only the quantity needed for the duration required to get the job done. To assist in this regard, United Rentals brings to market Total Control®, its telematics-enabled, fleet- and equipment-management system that provides visibility into both rented and owned equipment to improve utilization, maintenance and uptime.

Total Control® runs on Amazon Web Services. Data derived from connected machines in the field is collected into AWS and stored using many different technologies (SQL, NoSQL, flat file, etc.) in order to optimize the performance and data retention for the different customer use cases.

Data normalization occurs at the AWS gateway instance so data from different machines can be presented in a consistent way. For example, standard data formats are provided within the platform for different data types, such as analog values, discrete states or accumulators.

Aggregated data is generally stored for 13 months, after which the data is maintained in cold storage for longer periods and can be retrieved for larger analytics projects, contract or legal verification and more.

Precision Contractor

One Precision Contractor is part of a larger group that generates about $1.3 billion per year in revenue among all its companies. This company has done a number of major projects, including building a multi-million-dollar bridge, laying power cable to an offshore wind farm, and has either remodeled or built several water and waste treatment plants from the Midwest to the South.

In the early 2000s, the Precision Contractor had the foresight to build a custom hardware and software system to provide data from the construction machines used in the field. They decided to engineer their own system because no one at the time offered an off-the-shelf solution that provided telematics data (e.g., hours and location) along with fuel consumption.

All data from the company's fleet operating in the field is sent to its own datacenter located at its headquarters. Raw data is initially stored in a Microsoft SQL server database. The data is scrubbed once per day and then stored directly in a Viewpoint Vista ERP system. Logs are indexed to the individual machine level, which includes hour-meter data and idle time.

Employees can access data through an application sitting in the ERP database. They archive on a rolling, 12-month period, but have data back to the beginning of the project, roughly eight years ago.

JLG

Data coming off JLG's machines is initially collected at different clouds depending on the use case. For instance, JLG offers its own ClearSky platform—which runs on AWS—to manage its own fleets of equipment.

On the other hand, if the customer runs its own cloud environment for the management of its fleet, data can be collected in the customer's cloud via an API. For example, this is the case when connected JLG machines are run in the Precision Contractor's fleet.

Still, in other cases, data first goes to ORBCOMM's FleetEdge platform, which runs on a third-party private cloud in ORBCOMM's tier-two datacenter in Virginia. In this case data is stored in an Oracle Database Appliance running on EMC storage. Data is privately archived in short-term storage for about six months, at which point it's moved to a long-term archive.

IT service management data is collected in a custom application. JLG is planning to move to Baseplan in the future. Baseplan Software has been serving the industry since 1986, offering ERP software that has been specifically built for companies that manage groups of machines. Today, MAPICS is used for parts management, with AdONE as the parts forecasting tool. JLG has a custom application they call Service Bench, which has a deep integration with MAPICS to provide warranty management. Finally, JLG collects call-handling data using a Cisco system.

Takeuchi

Takeuchi offers its Takeuchi Fleet Management system for the management of its machines. At the machine level, TFM is implemented with ZTR Control Systems' (ZTR) telematics hardware that Takeuchi installs in its factory as part of the manufacturing process.

Data from connected Takeuchi machines is initially collected at ZTR servers, but Takeuchi pulls the data once a day through a standard API call. Data is then stored in a Microsoft SQL server database located at Takeuchi's data center. Data is archived for 18 months, and they have collected about 50GB of information to date.

Skanska

The Skanska inSite Monitor connects to the Microsoft Azure cloud. Sensor data is collected using Azure Table Storage, which is a NoSQL database for schemaless data storage. From there, data is processed by a cloud services worker role and transferred as structured data to an Azure SQL database, which also stores inSite Monitor configuration data such as names and locations of sensors. Also, when an alarm goes off, a record is generated and also saved to this SQL database.

Azure Blob Storage is available to store user data and image files, although at this time no user data is being stored—only icons for images. Blob Storage is Microsoft's object storage solution for the cloud, which is optimized for storing large amounts of unstructured data.

Oracle

Augmented reality is beginning to be used in the construction build and inspection processes. DAQRI's Smart Glasses™ transfer data to the Oracle IoT Cloud service—a PaaS offering. This enables device data from the field to be made available in real time for analysis and integration with enterprise applications, web services, and other Oracle cloud services such as Oracle Prime and Oracle IoT Connected Worker.

Collected data includes device statistics and analytics to improve the performance of the Smart Glasses™, along with device management data, such as what applications are installed on the device, and software patch levels. This data is stored indefinitely.

Sensor data is also collected in the Oracle IoT Cloud service, while camera video feeds are collected locally on the SSD. By default, DAQRI only stores sensor data required for the operation of its applications.

Next

Collection technology will be challenged in the future; we're going to need to find lower cost ways to store data coming from Things, as well as design faster processing architectures.

To get a sense of scale, suppose you have 100,000 machines in the field—which isn't outlandish, as United Rentals has over 425,000 machines deployed, and Vestas, the largest wind-turbine manufacturer, has at least 50,000. Let's assume you're only sampling data from your 100,000 machines once per hour and the amount of data is just 100 bytes. At that rate you'll generate 0.24GB of data per day, or 87GB per year. Let's assume you collect this data in a traditional database (such as Oracle, Microsoft, Pivotal, IBM or Teradata). If you took the average of the total cost of ownership of these five solutions from a recent report,[2] the cost of collecting the data would be approximately $16,000 per GB. For our IoT application, that would amount to $1.44 million.

Now let's suppose we keep the same number of machines but increase the data-sampling rate to once per minute. Again, this is not a wild assumption, as wind turbines today sample once every 5–10 seconds. Furthermore, let's assume we have more sophisticated sensors that now deliver 1,000 bytes of data. With just these two changes, the volume of data now moves to 144GB per day and 52,560GB (or 52 Terabytes) per year. At the same cost structures of about $16,000 per GB, a traditional collection approach would round out to $861 million for five years. This, of course, is if we only keep the data for one year and there are no new machines.

No matter how you slice it, we're clearly going to need lower-cost alternatives. But it's not just going to be about cost; traditional sequential techniques won't be adequate to process 52 Terabytes. Of course, the first question we might want to ask is how are we going to use the data? For the first time, we're going to get a lot of data without having to entice people to enter information manually—so what will we be able to learn?

---

[2] Microsoft Analytics Platform System Delivers Best TCO-to-Performance, published by: Value Prism Consulting; sponsored by: Microsoft Corporation, published September 2014

9

Learn Principles

With an increasing amount of data coming from Things, we'll need to apply technology to learn from the data. In this chapter, we'll cover some major areas including query technology, supervised and unsupervised machine learning and clustering.

At a high level, machine-learning algorithms can be divided into two distinct categories: supervised and unsupervised learning. Supervised-learning algorithms learn a predictive model that maps an input pattern to a desired output value. To train the predictive model in a supervised manner, we must use a set of training data consisting of input patterns together with the desired output values for each input pattern. The learning process is described as "supervised" because the predictive model is provided with supervisory information in the form of the true output values that it needs to predict during training.

In contrast, unsupervised learning is concerned with finding clusters in a set of input data and does not require any output values to be present in the dataset. Because, as an industry, we have mostly focused on IoP applications, most of the technology applied to learning from data streams has been applied to learning from data about people. In this chapter, we'll cover some of these basic concepts, some of which will apply to Things.

Database Query

A query is a specific request for a subset of data or for statistics about data, formulated in a technical language, and posted to a database system. Many tools are available to answer one-off or repeating queries about data posed by a worker. These tools are usually front ends to database systems based on SQL or a tool with a graphical user interface (GUI) to help formulate queries. For example, a query could answer the question: "Where are the most 100KW generators in the Northeast?"

Database queries are appropriate when you already have an idea of what might be an interesting subpopulation of the data and want to investigate this population or confirm a hypothesis about the data. In contrast, data mining could be used to come up with this query in the first place as a pattern or regularity in the data.

Online Analytical Processing (OLAP) provides a GUI to query large data collections for the purpose of facilitating data exploration. Unlike the ad-hoc querying enabled by tools like SQL, the dimensions of analysis for OLAP must be pre-programmed into the OLAP system. Unlike with OLAP, data-mining tools generally incorporate new dimensions of analysis easily as part of the exploration. OLAP tools can be a useful complement to data-mining tools for discovery from business data.

Prediction

At its most general, prediction is concerned with the task of estimating one or more desired quantities of interest (the "output values") given a number of input-data values, which are typically represented as a fixed-size vector. The job of the predictive model is to provide a mapping from the input-data vector to the desired output value(s). This mapping takes the form of a mathematical function, which is governed by a set of parameters, or weights. The job of the learning algorithm is to find the optimal set of parameters such that the predictive model is able to generate accurate predictions of the output values for each input vector that it's presented with.

The output values we wish to predict may be either continuous or discrete in nature. If the outputs are continuous values then the prediction problem is known as *regression* (the predictive model is known as a *regression model*). If the outputs are discrete values, then the prediction problem is known as *classification* (the predictive model is known as a *classifier*). To illustrate this further, consider two possible prediction problems when designing algorithms for a wearable fitness band. Predicting the heart rate of the user—a continuous value—would require a regression model. Conversely, predicting whether the user's heart-rate patterns were normal (class 0) or abnormal (class 1) would require a classifier.

Prediction, whether in the form of regression or classification, requires a *labeled* dataset to learn from. In a labeled dataset, each example is an input-output pair consisting of the input vector together with the desired output value (label). A supervised-learning algorithm uses this dataset to optimize the parameters of the predictive model, such that the model provides good predictive performance on new data. In order to assess the model's likely performance on new data, the labeled dataset is typically partitioned into a training set and a test set. The training set is then used to optimize the model parameters using a supervised-learning algorithm; and the test set is used to assess the model performance once training has completed.

Novelty Detection

Although predictive modeling is a powerful technique, there are problems where we would like to make a prediction about the state of a system, but where we are unable to apply the standard prediction techniques described in the previous section.

To illustrate, consider the task of predicting the health of a jet engine during flight. This type of problem is often referred to as *health monitoring* or *condition monitoring*. Specifically, we are tasked with building an algorithm that can predict if an engine is operating normally or, alternatively, operating in a novel or abnormal way that may indicate a problem within the engine. To approach this as a standard prediction problem, we would first collect a labeled dataset consisting of examples of jet engines operating normally (class 0) together with examples of engines operating abnormally (class 1). Given this dataset, we could then train a classifier in a supervised manner to decipher normal from abnormal engine behavior.

However, with this approach we quickly encounter a fundamental problem. What if we only have access to a very small number of examples of engines operating abnormally? In the extreme case, for a new model of a well-designed jet engine, we may not have any examples of the engine operating abnormally. In this scenario, our labeled dataset then consists solely of examples of engines operating normally.

Furthermore, even if we can obtain some examples of engines operating abnormally, we are still left with the problem that perhaps in the future, a fault may develop in some engines after many years of use that is quite different in nature to the abnormal examples present in our training set. So, we would like to be able to detect if an engine is operating abnormally, even when we may never have seen examples of this type of abnormal engine behavior during training.

The solution to this problem is a technique called *novelty* or *anomaly detection*. The key insight of the novelty detection approach is to focus exclusively on the *normal* data (i.e., the available data about the system behaving normally). Therefore, instead of trying to build a classifier to decipher normal from abnormal, we first build a model of only normal data. Then, using our "normality model," we test new input data against this model and evaluate the probability or likelihood that the data is indicative of the system operating normally (i.e., that the input data could have been generated by the normality model with high probability). If the normality model assigns high probability to the input data, we can be confident that the system is behaving normally; however, if the normality model assigns low probability to the data, then this is indicative of a potential problem because the input data is quite different from that which the model was trained on.

The power of this technique is that we are potentially able to detect novel or anomalous events in the data generated by complex systems—such as jet engines—when we may have never previously encountered examples of such events.

Clustering

Clustering is a set of techniques for discovering patterns or "clusters" within input data. A cluster is defined as a collection of input data vectors that are similar according to some metric. Most commonly, clusters refer to distinct regions of the input data space that have a high density of input data vectors such that the input vectors within each cluster can be considered to belong to some distinct underlying class or group. So, clustering is best viewed as a technique for discovering "groupings" within a dataset, which may not be readily apparent by computing simple, statistical summaries of the data.

Clustering is a form of unsupervised learning because it only uses the input-data vectors and does not make use of any labels or output values that we may have. It is distinct from novelty detection in that the aim of clustering is to discover groupings within the data where each grouping represents input patterns with high similarity; whereas the aim of novelty detection is to build a faithful, statistical model of the full range of normal input data.

A common use case for clustering is as part of an exploratory data analysis (EDA). EDA is often performed as one of the initial steps of a machine-learning project. Even when the overall aim of the project is to build a predictive model or a novelty detection system, it is often helpful to begin with a clustering and visualization stage in order to understand patterns in the data that may be helpful for subsequent modeling efforts.

Dynamic Machine Learning

For many machine-learning problems, we can consider that each data object in our dataset is *statistically independent* of all the other data objects in the dataset. For example, if we wish to predict the price of houses given data about each house (e.g., lot size, bedrooms, zip code, etc.), we can consider that each house is independent of the next. More precisely, the data about any given house does not provide useful predictive information about any other house. Intuitively this makes sense—the number of bedrooms (or lot size, heating type, etc.) in one house is unlikely to influence the price of another.

By treating the data—houses in this case—as independent of each other, we can represent each object by a fixed-size-feature vector and treat the set of feature vectors across all the data objects as independent of one another. This leads to conceptually simple machine-learning models that simply take a feature vector as input for a given data object and compute a desired value of interest (e.g., a class label, novelty score or cluster assignment).

However, for some important problems we cannot take that approach. For example, when analyzing a stream of time-series data from a sensor, we must consider the temporal patterns across the data in order to achieve optimal performance. If we attempt to "window" the time series to create a sequence of fixed-size-feature vectors that can be fed into a standard machine-learning model (e.g., a classifier), we are faced with a number of challenges such as how large to make our window (bigger equals more data for the features; smaller equals better temporal resolution), and how much to shift our window at each step. Furthermore, the resulting windowed feature vectors will likely exhibit significant correlations across one or more of the individual features; therefore, we need a way to model the statistical structure inherent in the time series. This is the domain of dynamic machine learning that is concerned with the analysis of sequence or temporal data for which the standard independence assumptions inherent in many machine-learning algorithms do not apply.

For time-series prediction problems, autoregressive models (and derivatives such as ARMA and ARIMA) provide a simple but effective form of dynamic machine-learning algorithm. For the most challenging problems, state-space models such as Kalman Filters and Hidden Markov Models (HMMs) can give superior performance.

Learning Lifecycle

It is tempting to view the learning process as a software-development cycle. Indeed, machine-learning projects are often treated and managed as engineering projects, which is understandable when they are initiated by software departments with data generated by a large software system and analytics results fed back into it. Managers are usually familiar with software technologies and are comfortable managing software projects; milestones can be agreed upon and success is usually unambiguous.

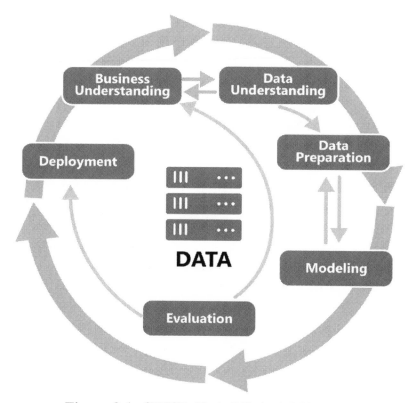

Figure 9.1: CRISP (Data Mining) Lifecycle

Software managers might look at the CRISP data-mining cycle (see Fig. 9.1) and think it looks comfortably similar to a software-development cycle, so they should be right at home managing an analytics or learning project the same way. This can be a mistake because learning is an exploratory undertaking closer to research and development than it is to engineering. The CRISP cycle is centered around exploration, iterating on approaches and strategy rather than software designs.

The task of determining a suitable representation of the raw input data that maximizes the performance of a machine-learning model is referred to as *feature engineering*, and the resulting data vector used as the input to the model is referred as a *feature vector*. Feature engineering is often one of the most important aspects of a machine-learning project. Coming up with good features that enable a machine-learning model to perform to a high standard on a given application requires a combination of exploratory data analysis, experimentation, and often the use of prior knowledge about the system under study.

Outcomes are far less certain, and the results of a given step may change the fundamental understanding of the problem. Engineering a learning or analytics solution directly for deployment can be an expensive, premature commitment. Instead, analytics projects should prepare to invest in information to reduce uncertainty in various ways. Small investments can be made via pilot studies and throwaway prototypes. Data scientists and machine-learning engineers should review the literature to see what else has been done and how it has worked. On a larger scale, a team can invest substantially in building experimental test beds to allow extensive agile experimentation. If you're a software manager, this will look more like research and exploration than you're used to, and maybe more than you're comfortable with.

Although machine learning involves software, it also requires skills that may not be common among programmers. In software engineering, the ability to write efficient, high-quality code from requirements may be paramount. Team members may be evaluated using software metrics, such as the amount of code written or number of bug tickets closed. In analytics, it's more important for individuals to be able to formulate problems well, prototype solutions quickly, make reasonable assumptions in the face of ill-structured problems, design experiments that represent good investments and analyze results. In building a data-science team, these qualities—rather than traditional software engineering expertise—are skills that should be sought.

Similar to what happened in traditional enterprise software, we're likely to see new analytic applications emerge, whether focused on a particular role or a specific vertical industry. For instance, new companies such TensorFlow and PyTorch are hiring data scientists and DevOps people to build analytic middleware.

Another good example is Lecida, the digital assistant for the enterprise. While Amazon, Google and Apple have developed digital assistants for the consumer, they are not relevant in the enterprise. To deliver the digital assistant, Lecida uses technologies such as large-scale cloud computing, deep learning and microservices from suppliers including ServiceMax, Amazon, Google, PTC and Twilio. The end user of the asset—maintenance, dealers, field service and engineering—can all use the assistant. Early customers have included companies across many industries, including construction, agriculture and power.

10

Learn in Practice

In the *Learn Principles* chapter we covered a few fundamental ways you can learn from the data coming from Things. Unlike the last generation of IoP applications, we don't have to wait for someone to buy a book or hire a new employee to have data to analyze. Machine-generated data is both richer (as we can have hundreds of sensors) and much more frequent (sometimes up to 60 times per second) than IoP data. As a result, there has been a great deal of work in technologies such as supervised and unsupervised machine learning, clustering, and engagement analysis.

We're still in the early stages, but this chapter will cover examples of learning in practice for key stakeholders in the construction industry—such as field foremen, purchasing agents and executives—to learn from data collected from their machines to better manage constructions projects.

Lead Time and Delivery

A key performance indictor (KPI) that United Rentals provides its customers is measuring and reporting on-time-delivery performance. This is important for two reasons. First, United Rentals provides its customers with an on-time-delivery guarantee for orders placed with a minimum of 72-hours' notice, meaning they need to track if they are in fact delivering equipment on time per this guarantee.

In addition, United Rentals can track if failure to deliver equipment on time is due to short lead-time requests by the customer. As such, United Rentals reports on-time delivery against four categories: less than 24-hours' notice, less than 48-hours' notice, less than 72-hours' notice and greater than 72-hours' notice.

This transparency with its customers holds United Rentals accountable for on-time deliveries while also showing customers how late-notice orders are impacting the on-time delivery of machines.

Location and History Mapping

United Rentals helps customers to know what is on rent and also provides history mapping. This capability allows customers to see any machine's last ten moves, displaying a marker on a mapping application that shows equipment make, model and number, along with position recorded by latitude and longitude. This not only provides the ability to map where rented equipment is located, but also see each machine's utilization and details about the rental transaction.

Utilization vs. Performance Benchmarks

One of the most important metrics to track is utilization against agreed-upon, benchmark-performance objectives. Utilization performance means actual hours used versus hours rented, while a performance benchmark represents an industry utilization benchmark, or a benchmark agreed upon at the start of a project.

United Rentals begins by providing its customers with a report that charts hours used per day, utilization for the last seven and last 30 days, and the current meter reading. In addition, United Rentals can provide a snapshot of actual utilization against agreed upon performance benchmark objectives. In supporting a solar energy project, for example, United Rentals showed how utilization dipped significantly when the project manager took his eye off the utilization numbers when he was gone for three weeks after his wife had a baby.

Alerts and Notifications

Running reports on past behavior has value, but one of the reasons why utilization can be enhanced for United Rentals customers is that alerts can be set up in Total Control® to send automated emails if a machine is sitting underutilized for a configurable number of days. Multi-tier alerts can also be set to notify various personnel if there is a lack of usage. Customers can also watch for pending and past-due alerts. These alerts allow customers to investigate underutilized machines relatively quickly and decide if they want to off-rent the equipment or start using them more.

The Human Element to Utilization

Managing utilization of operators and equipment is a big part of a construction project's costs, but it's not just reports that matter; there also needs to be the human element. One industry veteran explains that sometimes 40% idle time might be acceptable, as you might have a load on a boom lift that is holding some piece in place. The engine isn't on, but the machine is clearly being utilized.

Geo-fencing

Geo-fencing provides alerts when equipment leaves and returns to a virtually-fenced area. One use case for geo-fencing is the creation of an auto-rental yard where equipment can be virtually checked out and back in by simply moving in and out of the virtually-fenced area. This is an especially valued capability for secure job sites with heavily controlled access.

Service Calls

An important KPI to measure and report is service calls. Service calls include any machine issues, ranging from engine issues and tire problems to the air conditioning not working. For example, while supporting the solar energy project, United Rentals discovered that one common service call was repair requests for air conditioners. In fact, one site had eight broken A/C units over an approximate four-month period. At first glance this wasn't too surprising, given the construction site was immersed in over 100+ degree heat and 90% humidity.

But upon further investigation, it was discovered that all failures came from cabbed equipment that were being used by workers to cool down. The high utilization data from the running vehicles paired with the common issue of broken A/C units on those vehicles provided the red flag. However, more importantly, this insight provided an opportunity for the program team to discuss with the customer how to better manage onsite behavior to avoid unnecessary service costs.

Fundamental to the business, worker behavior needed to change because the general rental equipment was running two to three times the normal amount. This was not because the workers were using the machines to do work, but because they were using them to cool off despite the fact that there were dedicated cooling stations throughout the site. Therefore, using the cabbed equipment to keep cool produced a false reading of utilization in some cases because the team didn't know why the equipment was running. Was it digging, moving dirt, delivering materials on the project, or was the worker just eating lunch?

Machine Failure

Machine failure is almost always related to machine operations, such as the operator running a machine with an active error code. For example, if the engine begins to overheat on a Takeuchi connected machine, it will initially result in an audible alarm, flashing caution light, and an active error code present on the machine's display. As the machine continues to be operated while overheating, the active error codes, engine temperatures, run time and other useful diagnostic information is being stored in the Takeuchi Fleet Management system.

However, operators will often just restart the machine to clear the code even though it will continue to overheat, inevitably resulting in engine damage. Expensive repairs could be avoided if the operator shuts the machine down after the first alarm and repairs or discovers the cause of the overheating, such as low coolant or a dirty radiator.

In the days before machines were connected, the operator might have gone back to the dealer with a damaged machine, which would have to be covered under the two-year warranty period. Today, in the connected state, Takeuchi can more fully evaluate the circumstances of a failure when judged against the warranty. For example, if data shows that the operator ran the machine improperly or ignored error codes.

Operations and Regeneration

Takeuchi can use data to help operators learn how to better run their machines. For example, the conventional wisdom for operating diesel engines is to let them idle (i.e., don't ever shut them down). While that might have been true in the past, idling a Tier IV DPF-equipped diesel engine is one of the worst things one can do, as they don't burn as clean or as hot at idle. This can result in a prematurely clogged DPF. The problem with this is that the machine will either require more frequent regeneration or go into a state where the DPF will need to be removed and professionally cleaned. Regeneration will also be required more frequently if operators run their diesel engines with an average load rate of only 20% or less.

Regeneration is associated with diesel engines that are equipped with a diesel particulate filter (DPF). The DPF is a device designed to remove diesel particulate matter or soot from the exhaust gas of a diesel engine. As the filter becomes plugged it becomes restrictive and needs to be cleaned. Regeneration is the cleaning process that is used to burn off carbon particles in the exhaust filter. Most often the regeneration occurs automatically during normal operation without the operator even knowing. However, in some instances, the machine may require a parked regeneration, which requires the machine to be stationary while it completes this thorough cleaning to restore the effectiveness of the exhaust filter. Regeneration can last 30–45 minutes—all unproductive downtime.

Takeuchi machines have five alarm levels with regards to regeneration. At levels one and two there is a beep every 10 seconds, followed by the regeneration light illuminated on the operator's console. At level three there is a beep every second and an active error code, which requests the operator to stop the machine and do a regeneration. When level four is reached, the dealer has to come out to the field and force regeneration by connecting a laptop to the machine. And when a machine reaches level five, it's time to take the filter off and get it professionally cleaned. In any case, ignoring alerts can result in costly repairs.

Analytics Tools

Drawing insights from collected data can be benefited through the use of analysis tools. For its inSite Monitor device that monitors environmental variables such as vibration, noise and airborne particulates, Skanska uses Microsoft's Power BI toolset for data visualization. It allows Skanska to see its data organized in different kinds of charts and graphs, which in turn allows them to see trends. For example, Skanska can graph how the temperatures have been trending over the last hour or day or seven days. Skanska can also show various temperature information like current, max, min and average over the last 24 hours. In the future, Skanska plans to apply machine-learning algorithms to the stored data to search for and detect anomalies.

In order to detect if sensor values have gone beyond acceptable, normal parameters, Skanska uses Microsoft Azure Stream Analytics, a tool for querying data streams as they're happening in real time. Azure Stream Analytics uses a programming syntax similar to Transact-SQL (T-SQL). T-SQL is a set of programming extensions from Sybase and Microsoft that add several features to SQL. With this syntax, Skanska is able to write *SELECT* and *WHERE* statements to derive value from the data. For example, Skanska has written queries like "select where temperature is greater than X" or "select where humidity is greater than Y." In other words, as the data comes in, Skanska has written rules to detect anomalies and warning conditions in the data in real time.

Next

These examples provide a snapshot into what some companies are doing today to learn from machine data. However, one could argue that learning from connected construction machines is still in the early stages, as a higher level of analysis tools using machine-learning algorithms and artificial intelligence are yet to really be deployed.

That said, our biggest challenge in learning from machine data is people, not technology. Based on some analysis of enrollment for the machine-learning class at Stanford and other universities over the past ten years, you can extrapolate that there are probably only ten thousand people in the world trained in any form of machine learning.

Compare that number to an estimated ten million software programmers worldwide and you'll get an idea of the challenges, and perhaps more importantly, the opportunities.

11

Do Principles

Outcomes—what are they? What does all of this technology to connect, collect, and learn actually do? In this chapter, we'll discuss the value of higher degrees of service for machines, both to the producers and consumers of Things. As machines become more and more complex and increasingly enabled by software, many of the lessons learned in software maintenance and service will also apply to machine service. As many in the software industry already know, the movement to deliver software as a service has revolutionized the industry. We'll conclude by talking about how these software business models can reshape the business models for anyone building industrial products. These six outcomes are the business benefits for either the producers or consumers of modern machines.

But before we do that, let's discuss applications.

Enterprise Applications

Beginning in the late 1990s, a group of companies including PeopleSoft, Siebel, Oracle and SAP built enterprise applications on client/server architectures. These applications supported functions performed by people in finance, accounting, sales, marketing and human resources. And starting in the 2000s, many new companies such as Salesforce.com, NetSuite, Concur, Taleo and SuccessFactors emerged delivering similar functions as a cloud service. Specialized applications such as Veeva in pharmaceuticals, Dealertrack in automotive, and Blackbaud in philanthropy have also emerged.

Despite the success of these companies, packaged, enterprise applications cover a small percentage of what many enterprises do. A few years ago, Dr. Chou asked the CIO of 7-Eleven what percentage of the application footprint was bought from suppliers such as Microsoft or Oracle, and the answer was 10%. As a result, most enterprise applications are custom written. For example, 7-Eleven has a fuel-management application written for its gas stations.

Middleware

The term *middleware* has been classically used to describe a set of services or software that provides common functionality. A simple example is security services. All IoP applications need an authentication service to establish the identity of the individual. Managing the passwords, ensuring they are changed, and protecting the passwords are all common functions that don't need to be written by every developer. Another example is workflow or process management where common software can be used to orchestrate a step-by-step sequence of actions. You've seen a simple example of this every time you check out with your purchases on Amazon. While of course we could write a whole book on middleware, the intent of this chapter is to focus on some fundamental outcomes that would result from implementing an application. We'll begin with two important outcomes that machine providers might expect: improved quality and reduced cost of service.

Precision Machines: Improved Quality of Service

In the computing industry, both hardware and software companies have traditionally provided maintenance services. In the case of software, this is typically priced as a percentage of the initial purchase price; this business model generates the most revenue and profit. Many years ago, computer hardware companies connected their computers so they could "phone home" and report any potential problems, thereby improving the quality of service.

Of course, the manufacturers of generators, gene sequencers, and forklifts can do the same. By connecting their Things to the internet, not only are there potential additional revenue streams, but also the ability to provide better service, availability, security, performance and change management.

Better availability means less downtime for the customer; better performance management might mean telling the customer how to better use the machine; and better security means not only ensuring there aren't any viruses, but also notifying the customer when security patches are available for the software on the machine. And as so much of modern machines are made of software, better change management service will mean ensuring the customer knows there are new features available merely by upgrading their software. Based on usage data, equipment suppliers can suggest more appropriate models or companion equipment. All of us have seen Amazon provide personal and relevant information regarding other products that we might be interested in, so why not do the same things on the industrial side?

Precision Machines: Reduced Cost of Service

Traditional computer hardware service requires "rolling a truck" to bring spare parts to repair or service a machine. By connecting the machines, not only could you diagnose problems remotely, but also, if you need to make a house call you can ensure that you brought the right parts and tools for the job. All of this factors in to dramatically reducing the cost to deliver a service.

These principles are now available to the manufacturers of blood-diagnostic equipment, locomotives and wind turbines. By connecting these Things to the internet, manufacturers of machines can also reduce their cost of service. First, by being able to diagnose problems remotely and second, by ensuring that required parts are both available and arrive with the service technician, reducing repeat visits.

Maintenance of machines—whether that's high-speed inserters, 19-foot scissor lifts or HVACs—is often left as a cost to the purchaser. As consumers who have bought cars or computers, we know how true that is. A large construction rental company spends over one billion dollars per year on maintenance. General practice today is to implement time-based maintenance. As a driver, this means that every 12,000 miles you should put oil in your car. While this is the best we can do in a non-connected world, once we can connect many Things, it becomes possible to know the difference between a forklift that's been used in a sandy, humid, hot environment and one that's been in an air-conditioned warehouse for the past year. Being able to know precisely when the offshore wind turbines need service and being able to do that proactively has significant operational and economic benefit.

Precision Machines: New Business Models

Cisco released a report in early 2017 citing survey results that stated that close to three-fourths of all IoT projects are failing. The report goes on to say that part of the problem is a lack of interest from the top of companies, with leaders failing to "buy in" to IoT. Cisco's CEO then wrote, "We need to build IoT architecture that allows you to go beyond that 26 percent."

But we don't believe that more technology will convince CEOs to invest; instead, we need new business models. In this chapter, we'll make the case that as the manufacturer of construction, packaging, oil, gas, healthcare or transportation machines, you can double your revenues and quadruple your margins by building and selling digital service products. Furthermore, you'll create a barrier that your competition will find difficult to cross.

We'll cover three basic business models and discuss the organizational implications as well as some of the objections you'll encounter. These models provide a roadmap leading to digital transformation based on the experiences from the digital transformation of the enterprise computer hardware and software industry.

As an aside, a company's challenge to adopt digital transformation is often not a technical one. From our experiences working with many large and small IoT software companies, you can be assured the technology is available now or will be in the near future. Rather, a company's challenge is often organizational, bringing the executive team together to see the future.

Software-Defined Machine
Next-generation machines are increasingly powered by software. Porsche's latest Panamera has 100 million lines of code (a measure of the amount of software) up from only two million lines in the previous generation. Tesla owners have come to expect new features delivered through software updates to their vehicles. Healthcare machines are also becoming more software defined. A drug-infusion pump may have more than 200,000 lines of code, and an MRI scanner more than 7,000,000. A modern boom lift—commonly used on construction sites—has 40 sensors and three million lines of code, and a farm's combine harvester has over five million. Of course, we can debate if this is a good measure of software, but you get the point: software is beginning to define machines.

So, if machines are becoming more software defined, then maybe the business models that applied to the world of software will also apply to the world of machines.

Business Model 1: Product and Disconnected Services
Early on in the software-product industry we created products and sold them on a CD; if you wanted the next product, you'd have to buy the next CD. As software products became more complex, companies like Oracle and SAP moved to a business model where you bought the product (e.g., ERP or database) together with a service contract. That service contract was priced at roughly 2% of the purchase price

of the product per month. Over time, this became the largest and most profitable component of many enterprise software product companies. In the year before Oracle bought Sun Microsystems (when they were still a pure software business), they had revenues of approximately $15 billion, only $3 billion of which was product revenue, the other $12 billion (over 80%) was high-margin, recurring-service revenue.

But what is service? Is service answering the phone nicely from Bangalore? Is it flipping burgers at McDonald's? The simple answer is no. Service is the delivery of information that is personal and relevant to you. That could be the hotel concierge telling you where to get the best Szechwan Chinese food in walking distance, or your doctor telling you that, based on your genome and lifestyle, you should be on Lipitor. Service is personal and relevant information.

We've heard many executives of companies who make machines say, "Our customers won't pay for service." Well, of course, if you think service is break-fix, then the customer clearly thinks you should build a reliable product. Remember Oracle's service revenue? In 2004, the Oracle Support organization studied the 100 million requests for services from Oracle support and over 99.9% of those requests were answered with known information. Aggregating information for thousands of different uses of the software, even in a disconnected state, represented huge value over the knowledge of a single person in a single location. Service is not break-fix. Service is relevant information about how to maintain or optimize the availability, performance or security of the product.

In the world of machines, you might wonder why General Electric is running ads on Saturday Night Live that address the Industrial Internet. To get the answer, all you need to do is download GE's 2016 10-K and look on page 36. Out of $113 billion in revenue, they recognized $52 billion (nearly 50%) as service revenue. Imagine if GE could move to 80% service revenue. Not only would the company be tens of billions of dollars larger, but also the margins for the overall business could easily double. And let us remind you that this is all done without connecting the product (software or machine). If you're the CEO of a power, transportation, construction, agriculture, oil and gas, life science or healthcare-machine company, ask yourself: How big is my digital service business?

Business Model 2: Product and Connected Services
Of course, if you could connect to the product, you could make the service even more personal and relevant. Many software and hardware product companies connect to their products and provide assisted services. These services assist IT workers in maintaining the security, availability and performance of the product (e.g., database, middleware, financial application), and help them to optimize or improve it.

Now let's move to the world of machines. If a company knows both the model number and current configuration of the machine, as well as the time-series data coming from hundreds of sensors, then the service can be even more personal and relevant and allows the company to provide precision assistance for workers who maintain or optimize the performance, availability and security of the machine.

Let's assume you build this digital service product and price it at 1% of the purchase price of the software. If your company sells a machine for $200,000 and you had an installed base of 4,000 connected machines, you could generate $100 million of high-margin, recurring revenue. Companies who have moved to just 50/50 models (50% service and 50% product) have seen their margins quadruple.

Business Model 3: Product-as-a-Service
Once you can tell the worker how to maintain or optimize the
security, availability or performance of the product, the next step is to
simply take over that responsibility as the builder of the product. Over
the last fifteen years we've seen the rise of Software-as-a-Service
companies (SaaS) such as Salesforce.com, Workday and Blackbaud,
which all deliver their products as a service. In the past seven years,
this has also happened with hardware products as companies like
Amazon, Microsoft and Google provide compute and storage
products as a service.

All of these new product-as-a-service companies have also changed
the pricing to a per-transaction, per-seat, per-instance, per-month or
per-year model. We're likely to see the same with agriculture,
construction, transportation and healthcare machines. Early examples
we're all familiar with are Uber and Lyft, which provide
transportation machines as a service, priced per ride. Of course, the
most expensive operating cost is the human labor, so like those of us
in high-tech software and hardware products, they are looking at
replacing the human labor with automation. Note that this is the same
thing we had to do to deliver software, compute and storage as a
service.

In the end, the traditional car manufacturers all have to respond. The
replacement of Ford's CEO is the most recent visible example in the
transportation industry, which brings us to change management and
leadership.

Chief Digital Services Officer
While we have mostly focused on a discussion of digital service
products, you must also appreciate that there are significant
organizational changes that must be made if you adopt this strategy.

Many senior managers of aviation, construction and healthcare equipment companies are trained and focus on the design and production of the physical product, not software or services. Consider creating a chief services officer as a member of your leadership team and ensuring that a VP of digital service products and of digital service sales and marketing reports to them.

There will be obstacles, many of which will be internal, while some will be the channels to market. First, your VP of engineering will wonder why you're taking the R&D budget down; he would much rather build you more horsepower and torque in your next machine. Your VP of sales will question the wisdom of moving from a one-time, product-revenue model to a recurring-service model. How will the sales force be compensated? Local distributors who have relied on one-off, human-powered services will also object. General-purpose service companies, facilities managers in the building industry, or outsourcers in the tech industry will also see this as a threat. All of this can cause you to delay the implementation. But if history is an indicator, by the time your competitors have made the transition, it will be too late.

So, if you build machines for transportation, power, water, agriculture, construction, oil and gas or healthcare, hopefully you can now see a roadmap. This roadmap is based on the experiences from the digital transformation of the enterprise computer hardware and software industry. We know from working with numerous large and small IoT software companies that you can be assured that we have or will have the technology. Your challenge as the CEO is to bring your executive team together to see the future.

While the journey will not be easy, the rewards of having a high-margin, recurring-revenue, differentiated product will enable you to thrive in the coming decade.

Let's now switch gears from machine-building enterprises to those that *use* machines. For an enterprise that uses machines to provide a service, there are three major outcomes of connecting and learning from those machines.

Precision Service: Lower Consumables Cost

Many machines consume materials during operations. This could be fuel in the case of an airplane, ink for a high-speed printer, or chemical reagents in a gene sequencer. These consumables often form a large portion of the operational cost structure. As anyone with an inkjet printer knows, the cost of the printer is not your operational cost. At the enterprise level in the airline industry, the single largest operational cost is fuel—in some cases that's nearly 30% of the total.

By connecting machines to the internet and learning from them, operators can make different decisions on how to drive the train or configure the printer to optimize the consumption of fuel, ink or energy.

Precision Service: Higher Quality Product or Service

As the operator of a utility, farm or airline, connecting your Things, collecting the data and learning from them should also improve the precision of your operations. In the case of agriculture, this could mean higher quality products with lower impact on the environment.

Precision agriculture not only means using GPS to make sure you're only going over each row once with your fertilizer, but also using fewer herbicides, the right amount of water, and harvesting at the peak time based on data.

Precision Service: Improved Health and Safety

The derailment of an Amtrak train in Philadelphia in 2015 left at least six people dead and created chaos on the heavily traveled Northeast Corridor the next morning, cutting off all direct rail service between Philadelphia and New York City and causing major delays up and down the East Coast. Connecting trains, learning from the data, and advising the human operator or taking over the train (as Rio Tinto is on track to do in 2018 for iron ore trains) will not only reduce operation costs, but also improve safety. With so many accidents caused by cell phone use, you have to wonder if autonomous cars will be safer. As another example, in some manufacturing, mining and construction sites, performing real-time tracking of workers and equipment in order to issue alerts when they move into dangerous areas would be simple with connected machines.

Summary

While technology is cool, its real usage has been to transform businesses. We're all familiar with the examples from the consumer space (Google, Uber, eBay), but IoT technology has the potential to do the same for producers and consumers of the machines used in agriculture, healthcare, power, transportation, water and more. These next-generation applications are likely to look completely different. For example, enterprise asset management defined by companies like

Maximo is based on the idea that the machines are dumb and not connected. Companies like Oomnitza have emerged which assume tomorrow's machines are as smart as today's cell phones. So they are taking the software they built to manage cell phones and laptops and repurposing it to manage the machines of the future.

For a manufacturer of Things, technology can not only reduce the cost and improve the quality of service, but also deliver new revenue sources from new business models. As an operator of this next generation of Things, you have the ability to use precision machines to deliver higher quality and lower cost food, power and water, and safer and lower cost transportation and healthcare.

12

Do in Practice

We're still in the very early stages of seeing what IoT technology will do for manufacturers of machines and those who use them. General Electric has done some analysis of a 1% change in the industries they serve. For instance, for a precision manufacturer of oil and gas machines, an improvement in machine availability by 1% would save nearly $7 billion per year. For a precision airline or utility, a 1% savings in fuel across the industry would result in $2–3 billion in savings per year. Likewise, in the power industry, a 1% savings in fuel would add up to nearly $5 billion in annual savings.

While these are industry wide estimates, we'll explore a few cases that quantitatively and qualitatively illustrate the implications in the construction industry. At the end of the chapter we'll talk about some of the qualities we might see in next-generation IoT applications and middleware.

Precision Machines

Reporting Optimal Utilization

Analysis of data helps JLG and its rental-company customers and contractors to understand true utilization—both actual and optimal—of the machines in the field. Actual utilization reports if a machine is sitting idle at a job site or is being transported—indicated by full-wheel-drive activity moving through a site and over certain distances. On the other hand, optimal utilization includes, for instance, reporting if a machine is being run out of spec, over speed, beyond a tilt angle, or operated in an unsafe manner.

Improving Machine Availability

Before its machines were connected, Takeuchi would see some kind of failure about six times a year. These failures were due to things like dirty air filters, dead batteries and operator misuse. With connected machines, there are now significant improvements to machine availability. This means the owner of the machines—such as the rental agency or contractor—has the information needed to stay on top of maintenance. Keeping equipment maintained helps to keep the machines running so the contractor can get the job done on time and on budget.

Reducing Maintenance Costs

Takeuchi and others also provide the ability to diagnose a connected machine. This can save the contractor who uses the machines a hefty bill to have a tech come out to the site. Customers often call in and say that a machine is beeping and they don't know what to do. With Takeuchi Fleet Management, the owner of the machine can see, for instance, that the machine just needs a regeneration and can then walk the operator through that procedure. If they have to roll a truck to the machine, the customer is looking at a $500–$1,000 charge.

Predictive Maintenance

Many of JLG's biggest customers are rental companies, so a machine that can't be rented is a loss for the company; therefore, predictive maintenance reports are a big deal. Utilizing data for predictive maintenance not only means telling the customer that, based on usage, it's time to change the equipment's oil, but it also means the ability to predict potential errors depending on the error codes across the customer's entire fleet of JLG equipment. With JLG's ClearSky platform you can see when the last maintenance was performed as well as the next scheduled maintenance. In the future, JLG hopes to use the sensor data to recommend service based on actual utilization and the performance of specific machines such as boom and scissor lifts.

Understanding Total Cost of Ownership

JLG uses data obtained from its machines in the field to understand total cost of ownership. For any particular machine, JLG knows what type of duty cycle it's operated on and what kind of use and abuse it suffered. Therefore, based on the type of maintenance required, the age of the machine, the cost of the machine, the types of replacement parts a customer has purchased, the cost of operations of a given machine, and relative values compared to the rest of their fleet, JLG can determine how much the machine costs to stay up and running. This overall picture reveals if it's financially worth it to keep up a particular machine or sell it and buy a new one. JLG also uses this information to send recommendations back to the rental agencies as to when maintaining a machine is no longer cost effective.

New Business Models

Connecting machines also allows for new business models. TALISMAN Rentals charges customers for the hours of run time instead of just the number of days they have the machine. And

Takeuchi provides its fleet-management service as part of its initial, two-year, 2,000-hour warranty period. Once they go off warranty, TFM is an optional service.

Precision Contractors

Increasing Machine Utilization
Increasing utilization of machines, either rented or owned, is clearly in the best interest of the contractor. United Rentals was demonstrating its Total Control® fleet management system to a major electrical contractor customer when a $5,000/month excavator the customer had on rent came up as not having been moved in over two months. The contractor's CFO was shocked and immediately called the foreman on the job site. The foreman reported that the job had been delayed so the machine hadn't been used, but it was going to be used again "soon." Within the hour, the CFO wanted to review the data again and to everyone's surprise the excavator no longer displayed. It turns out, immediately after the call, the foreman had quickly gone and off-rented the excavator.

Reducing Machines Rented and Additional Operators
One construction company reduced the number of scissor lifts it rented from ten to seven by rescheduling work after seeing data provided by Total Control®. Another company reduced its number of machines from 15 to 7. In both cases, not only did the customer reduce their overall rental costs but they also didn't have to pay for the additional operators. On the other hand, there was a customer who had no visibility into the usage of the machines it owned. In response, United Rentals installed portable Slap Track devices on 300 of the customer's owned equipment and measured utilization over a period of about three months. It turns out the company was using its owned

equipment with only about 10% utilization compared to the equipment rented from United Rentals. As a result, the customer sold off 270 pieces of its own equipment.

Ensuring Machine Utilization is Getting Work Done
One United Rentals customer was showing high utilization rates, and a closer look at the data showed that operators where spending a large percentage of their time traveling from location to location within the job site. An even deeper examination revealed that there was a location on the job site where people were often spending 10–20 minutes, which looked like very short-duration work. Other times, the equipment was there for 45 minutes before moving to another location. In addition, there was a wide variety of equipment stopping at this particular location, but interestingly a vast majority was operator-run equipment like forklifts and backhoes. It turned out this location was being used as a smoke pit. The machines were indeed being used, but as transportation for operators to go spend an average of 15–30 minutes to smoke cigarettes.

Precision Billing through Geo-fencing
One challenge, especially at larger job sites, is distributing and assigning rental costs. Construction companies prefer a rental charge be not only charged to the job site, but also further broken down to a particular building or maintenance facility. Total Control® enables this through geo-fencing. With geo-fencing, when the customer gets a bill from United Rentals, they're able to take that bill and distribute it across the different cost centers. The geo-fencing capability also enables "mod yards." Mod yards are commonly seen in Canada where building units are pre-assembled and taken to the site with minimal on-site construction required. In these cases, there are often several types of projects going on within a large area with equipment being rented full time but shared across the various projects. The customer

wants to track where the rented equipment is being used so rental charges can be assigned based on usage by project.

Best Practices

One best practice deployed by United Rentals includes sharing weekly reports with the contractor's executive staff and project managers. This provides the contractor with visibility—mid-month or mid-bill cycle—into fuel discussions. With a common view of the data, the United Rentals team uses these discussions to address service issues, utilization, exchanges and upcoming rentals. They also talked about the opportunities to off-rent various machines based on their overall utilization for the last month. Project managers use the data from Total Control® to see outliers in the data and then investigate those on site in order to make better utilization decisions. Essentially focusing on the issues rather than on what's going well— something United Rentals calls 'management by exception.'

Reducing Theft and Enhancing Safety

A big challenge for companies like the Precision Contractor is that the same physical key can start all equipment from a particular manufacturer. For example, a particular John Deere key will start up *any* piece of John Deere equipment within a certain year range, regardless of which company owns the unit. This is the same situation with CAT, Komatsu and many others. This creates the vulnerability that very expensive equipment can more easily be stolen. In fact, a disgruntled ex-employee once stole an excavator from a job in the hills of Kentucky and proceeded to drive the $300,000 piece of equipment up a mountaintop and down the other side where he promptly set it on fire.

Using traditional keys to start equipment also means there are no safeguards in place as to who can start up and run a piece of equipment, which introduces safety risks as well. For instance, if a group of kids were to happen upon a construction site and find a key that enabled them to start equipment, it could be a very tragic day if someone got hurt.

In response, the contractor gave Honeywell HID security cards to operators and added readers to equipment that tie to the specific machines. Cards are assigned to individual, active employees. On the back-office side, the company ties the completion of training to an operator's security card so only those with the proper training and credentials for that specific model of machine are able to start it. This not only limits the ability for just any employee to start and run any machine, but it also prevents theft, as ex-employee access privileges can be immediately terminated.

Operator Performance Tracking
Connecting the machine and the operator also allows for operator-performance tracking. Because it is now known precisely *who* started up and ran a particular piece of equipment, usage can be tied directly back to the operator. Companies can track individual operator run and idle time, thus individual performance, versus only knowing machine utilization regardless of who actually ran the equipment. Additionally, without connectivity, companies have to manually match up time cards or payroll entries with equipment usage.

Tracking operator performance is much less about a contractor playing the role of Big Brother, and more about reducing idle time by better coaching its operators. For example, by looking at an operator's idle-time performance over five different machines, a company can know how well he does at managing utilization. And if he does a poor job, the company is able to coach him.

Identifying Culprits in Damaged Equipment Cases
Utilizing HID cards also helps to address the issue of equipment damage that often goes unreported. Now, a company can narrow the list of potential suspects by knowing who started the machine during the period of time when the machine was damaged. With HID cards the contractor can run a report and boil it down to a few people, enabling them to identify the culprit from there.

Packaged IoP Applications

Just as with the Internet of People, we'll see packaged applications like financials, ERP, CRM and HR applications for the Internet of Things. While there may not be many horizontal applications, one example Thing might be asset-, machine- and device-management. A Thing-management application differs from IoP applications in significant ways.

For one, it's engineered and delivered as a cloud service. Just hosting traditional asset management applications (like IBM's Maximo) is not the same as engineering them from the ground up to be cloud-based apps. Just compare Siebel to Salesforce or Exchange to Gmail to understand the difference.

It's also architected around Things, not people. We've already made the point that Things are not people. Asset-management applications and service-management applications (like ServiceNow) are people-centric, not Thing-centric.

In addition, it's architected around smart, connected Things. Last-generation asset management assumed you walked around and inventoried the assets. You had to be physically close. Next-generation Thing management assumes you can find the Thing (asset, machine, or device) on the network.

Additionally, Things are smart. In the IoP world, people issue trouble tickets, but when there is a 1GHz microprocessor in all our Things, why not have our Things issue the trouble tickets?

Also, Things are connected. Traditional applications are only focused on a single Thing owned and maintained by a company. These are typically deployed on premise and never engineered to connect to the internet. For example, you'd never be able to know the resale value of your generator, blood analyzer or gene sequencer in the global market—something we can easily do today with any consumer product.

And finally, it's engineered for security and privacy. While every application has some authentication and access control, most traditional asset-management and service-management applications never expected the level of threats in the network nor found ways to manage and control them.

Next-Generation Middleware

Custom, industry-specific applications dominated the last generation of enterprise applications (as few applications are truly horizontal), and the next generation promises to be no different. If this is the case, we're going to need a middleware layer. While some extension of existing IoP middleware that supports security, workflow or user-interface design has emerged, this will be inadequate for IoT applications for many reasons.

For example, first consider that security for IoT applications must be bi-directional. Not only do you need to manage the identity and credentials of Things and their access to the system (i.e., protect the system against the Things), you also need to manage the credentials for the system to access each of the Things (i.e., protect the Things against the system).

You must also consider machine data versus nomic data. AGCO talks about the "two-pipe" approach, but we're going to need to be able to control and secure data about the fertilizer-spraying machine from the agronomic data, or data about the reagents in a blood-analysis machine from blood-analysis results. This has never been true about IoP applications.

Also, much of IoP middleware is based on the idea of transaction integrity. In the event of a failure, you roll back the transaction; the physical world runs on the time axis and time does not roll backwards.

And finally, consider that Things won't use UIs. Things only follow concrete procedures defined by their internal mechanics. Such requirements call for a much more sophisticated interaction framework between Things and the application.

We're in the very early stages of this third generation of enterprise software, but you can already see early signs of how software promises to change both the manufacturers of machines and the many industries that use those machines to deliver the services the planet depends on.

13

Summary – Principles and Practices

IoT could easily represent the third major generation of enterprise software and hardware technology. You can go to the internet and find many projections about how big IoT is going to be. Given that the first two generations of enterprise software have basically just automated some back-office functions (e.g., HR, payroll and financials) and have left the fundamental businesses untouched, you might agree that IoT may hold the promise to actually transform fundamental businesses.

As in other technology markets, the IoT market will have a variety of players and strategies. Some suppliers will compete by offering distinctive technology, while others will offer distinctive data. Some will try to be platform plays, both through organic investment and acquisitions, and others will still focus on a particular product space. And still, others will offer technology consulting and services to put all of the pieces together.

So the question we raise is: Why are these IoT products and services not merely an extension of the first and second-generation products? The simple and obvious answer is that Things aren't people. All of the technology built to date has been to build IoP, not IoT, applications. While all of the stories in this book are using current technology, what is in front of us will look significantly different.

IoT applications differ from IoP applications in three fundamental ways.

First, there are a lot more Things than people. These days, you can't be on the internet without seeing some pronouncement of how many things are going to become connected. John Chambers, former CEO of Cisco, recently declared there will be 500 billion Things connected by 2024; that's nearly 100 times the number of people on the planet.

Second, Things can tell you more than people. A keyboard is the major mechanism used by people to tell an application something, and most applications use some type of form to collect simple amounts of data from individuals. Things have many more sensors; a cell phone has nearly 14 sensors, including an accelerometer, GPS and even a radiation detector. Industrial Things like wind turbines, gene sequencers or high-speed inserters can easily have more than 100 sensors.

And finally, Things can talk constantly. Most of the data from IoP applications comes from either encouraging us to buy something or making it part of the hiring process. In short, people don't enter data frequently into an e-commerce, HR, purchasing, CRM or ERP application. On the other hand, a phase measurement unit can send data 60 times per second; a high-speed inserter can send data once every two seconds; and a construction forklift can send data once per minute.

Sensors continue to drop in price and increase in functionality. James Park, founder and CEO of Fitbit, once commented in Dr. Chou's Stanford class that we're getting to the point where some devices, formally thought of as only available in the hospital setting, can be brought to a consumer price point. Connection technology has largely been based on people randomly communicating from people-friendly locations. If we have constant communication from many more locations around the planet, what new connection infrastructure could emerge? How will we build communication networks that stream from Things back to the cloud?

Historically, we've collected data in SQL databases, but while we've built larger ones, put them in memory, etc., we know that the overhead of providing transaction integrity and the ability to equally read and write data is huge. There are already alternatives that are one-tenth the cost to collect the data. Of course, all of this data will be stored and managed as a cloud service, avoiding the cost and unreliability of the handcrafted, on-premise solutions.

Once data is collected (and we can collect a lot more), our traditional business-intelligence technologies are inadequate. While machine learning has been used in certain applications, there is the opportunity to bring it to a much wider audience. And as we've seen in the last generation, there will need to be middleware that can provide IoT application programmers with the tools and services to quickly and reliably build applications.

There will be both technical and organizational challenges, particularly the increased concern and reality of a hostile world where shutting down the power grid could be as catastrophic as the bombing of Pearl Harbor. As a result, every component of the framework will need to provide security features. Security will need to evolve to be on an equal footing with product features. So, what's a security feature?

Hardening a machine means you have all good software and no bad software. So, providing a compute and storage cloud service not only includes all of the software management, but also the delivery of the compute and storage service, plus all of the software in the data center, power management and building access.

Recognizing this, let's focus on just one aspect: having all good software. Every vendor releases security patches on a regular and (sometimes) emergency basis. In a particular compute and storage cloud service this could easily translate to hundreds of patches per quarter.

Imagine a cloud service provider saying:

> *"Within 92 minutes, +/- 5 minutes of the release of all security patches, we perform 1,124 tests and place the patch into production within 22 hours, +/- 10 minutes."*

What if a machine provider could say the same thing?

Technology is built, sold and delivered by people. One of our biggest challenges will be education on new technologies and increasing our understanding of the domains of healthcare, mining and water treatment. In technology today, the world has about ten million programmers, but a back-of-the-envelope analysis says there are probably only ten thousand people who have ever had a basic education in machine learning. With the potential to collect so much data, we'll have to meet the challenge of educating a new generation. It won't just be education on connection, collection or learning technology—it will also be education on the domains. In the past year, we have learned an amazing amount about farming, high-speed printing and gene sequencers. We have seen that it will be paramount to find a way to have our technologists understand more about the domains, and for domain experts to be able to speak the language of the technologists.

While there are many more challenges—seen and unseen—this area remains one where the opportunity for innovation is high and the impact on both the planet and people's lives might be much greater than we've seen so far. We will need more precision technology to build precision machines for the sake of providing precision services to the world.

Part 2: Solutions

14

Introduction – Solutions

Part 1 described the fundamental technologies required to build Internet of Things applications. Part 2 provides a number of cases demonstrating how enterprises are currently adopting these technologies. You'll find the stories are told from different points of view—from either the companies that make, rent, or use construction machines. We'll explore a wide range of applications, from those that leverage traditional telematics to those that are automating the machines and using virtual reality to visualize the entire construction process.

All of the stories are organized around the Precision Framework (Things, Connect, Collect, Learn and Do), which we discussed in Part 1.

In addition, all of these stories were designed to be applicable for both technologists and business people, as well as for suppliers, buyers and stakeholders at the construction site, such as supervisors, procurement managers and the executive team.

Figure 14.1: Precision Framework

Things
Whether we're describing next-generation construction machines that come out of the factory enabled to connect to the network or talking about retrofitting existing equipment, the *Things* section will describe what the Thing is and what kind of data is being sensed. We'll show you a lot of specific examples from scissor lifts and environmental monitoring to augmented reality glasses and a brick-laying robot.

Connect

This section describes how the machines are connected. In some examples, we'll discuss both the network layer (typically via WiFi, MiFi or 3G), as well as the transport layer (e.g., AMQP), and in some stories we will also discuss how the connection is secured between the Thing and the cloud.

Collect

Once connected, there are various ways the data can be collected, ranging from SQL and time-series databases to NoSQL implementations. This section discusses the technology being used, how much data is being stored, and decisions around frequency and duration of archiving or retention.

Learn

Everyone is trying to analyze and learn from data, whether that's learning how to locate a machine, understanding how often it is being utilized, or knowing if the plumbers are planning to run pipe where electrical wiring is supposed to go. Each of the stories will cover what applications are being used to analyze and draw insights from the data.

Do

Finally, what should you *do* with what you've learned? We'll share many examples of how precision technology is helping make the construction site more productive and safer while also reducing costs. Whether it's helping contractors avoid renting equipment they don't really need or making sure operators are only starting equipment they are trained on and have permission to run, we'll discuss the value received by deploying precision technologies.

As you read these stories you may discover a subtle—or not so subtle—conversation that emerges around what "service" is in a world of networked machines and tools running analytics over machine-generated data. In the traditional view of the world, service is equated with "break-fix" and customers are reluctant to pay for this type of service because they expect the manufacturer to deliver machines that don't break. On the other hand, once we connect our machines, services can be offered that deliver insights about how to best operate the construction site based on machine data. This type of service can be valued in a completely different way.

For instance, in the Precision Solar Energy Project story, we discover that over $900,000 in rental costs was saved on a $7 million project. The contractor customer was able to save this money because its supplier of construction machines—United Rentals—was able to very precisely coach them on how to increase utilization by only renting what the data showed was needed at the construction site. Of course, this level of service offered by United Rentals far surpasses "break-fix."

In addition, as you read through the construction stories, you might notice another related conversation: Who should offer this new generation of services to the contractors? Should the OEM provide this next generation of connected services because they know best how to efficiently run their equipment? In fact, they have the potential advantage of aggregating data from their machines being run all around the world in all kinds of environments. Or should the rental agency offer the service, given they are providing a fleet of different OEM equipment to meet the contractor's overall needs on a project-by-project basis?

The answer is still in the planning stages. That said, one thing that struck us over and over again when writing these stories was how compelling the next generation of services is to the stakeholders at the construction site. In other words, whether you're a manufacturer of construction equipment or a rental agency, why wouldn't you at least explore what value-added services you can provide your customers to help them stay on schedule and on budget? Likewise, if you're a stakeholder at a construction site, why wouldn't you use connected machines so you can better enable yourself to stay on time and on budget while also providing a safer environment for your employees?

With this line of thought, the answer to who will ultimately offer the next generation of services may first be decided by who is late to the precision party—the laggards who find out too late that the competition already left them in the dust.

15

Precision United Rentals

United Rentals (UR) was founded in 1997 and is the largest equipment rental company in the world, with locations in 49 states and 10 Canadian provinces, and now with 11 locations in Europe. As a renter of equipment, UR focuses on driving operational efficiency and excellence in equipment delivery. Like a systems integrator, UR pulls together multiple platforms and manufacturing tools and prepares them for delivery to its customers in a ready state. This means making sure equipment is fueled, cleaned, operational, charged and delivered on time.

One of UR's main objectives is to help customers save money by more effectively managing rental consumption; in other words, renting only the quantity needed for the duration required to get the job done. At first glance this might seem counterintuitive for an equipment-rental company, but putting the customer first creates valuable long-term loyalty.

One person driving this quest to put the customer first is Mike Bierschbach, director of fleet technology and intelligence. Mike and his team are on the ground delivering solutions to customers that increase utilization and, ultimately, save them money.

Total Control® represents one such solution. Total Control® is UR's telematics-enabled fleet- and equipment-management system that provides visibility into both rented and owned equipment to improve utilization, maintenance and uptime.

But before this value could be fully delivered to its customers, UR's existing rental fleet of 450,000+ pieces of non-connected construction equipment had to be retrofitted with networked, telematics capabilities—no easy task. But Mike and his team were up for the challenge.

Things

United Rentals' customers were saying: If you can get 12-volt power off of the machine either by engine or battery, then we want telematics on it. Given UR can keep equipment in its fleet for seven to nine years, a strategy of waiting for the entire fleet to turn over with newly purchased telematics-enabled equipment would take six or more years to accomplish. This was too long considering the plan was to have Total Control® available for everybody, everywhere in less than two years.

Therefore, Mike and his team had to develop a retrofit strategy for the 450,000+ pieces of equipment spread across the US and Canada, approximately 70% of which are always out on rent. Also, given that rental customers often have their own fleets, UR's retrofit strategy had to work for customer-owned equipment so Total Control® could monitor the entire fleet on a job site. Finally, the strategy had to be compatible with newly acquired telematics-enabled equipment coming from OEMs.

To help solve this challenge, UR partnered with Sam Hassan and his team at ZTR Control Systems (ZTR), a telematics company founded in 1987 from a team of engineers that worked in the locomotive industry.

They engineered three edge solutions depending on the type of machine to be connected and the primary use case:

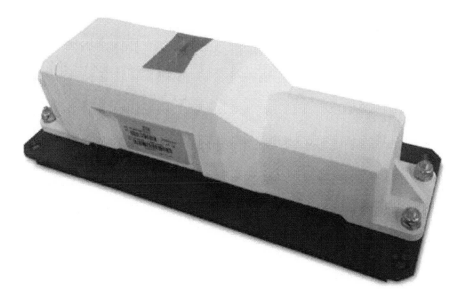

Figure 15.1: Portable "Slap Track" Device

Temporary: A portable "Slap Track" device, as shown in Fig. 15.1, is a small and simple unit that attaches to a machine to provide location and an estimate of run hours based on vibrations. This device is predominately deployed for short-term installs.

This M4 solution has a lithium-ion-based battery that can supply up to five years of life transmitting data multiple times per day as well as tracking the motion hours of the machine. The solution utilizes a 4G LTE Cat 1 cellular-based radio with a 56-channel GPS receiver. The device is IP-67 and completely self-contained with battery, GPS, and communications in one package, making it easy to install and able to withstand harsh work environments.

Figure 15.2: Retrofit Device

Retrofit: This M6 device by ZTR, shown in Fig. 15.2, provides basic machine connectivity giving visibility into run hours, location, battery level, low battery voltage alerts, fuel level and output control. The device utilizes a 4G LTE Cat 1 cellular radio with a 3G HSPA fallback. GPS is provided by a 56-channel GPS receiver and internal antennas for both GPS and cellular needs.

The M6 was built to adapt to various retrofit applications and can be mounted in various locations, is IP-66 rated and powered by 12-volt and 24-volt battery systems. With internal antennas and a harness with connector solution, the M6 is an easy to install and supportable solution.

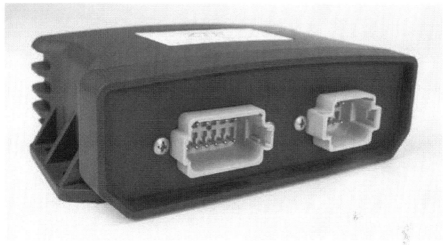

Figure 15.3: M8 Advanced Monitoring Device

New OEM Advanced Monitoring: The M8LZT, shown in Fig. 15.3, provides advanced connectivity and monitoring that integrates into the equipment's CAN bus J1939 network to provide run hours, location, engine data, machine faults, emissions data, regeneration status, fuel level, and other machine sensor data. The M8LZT comes with optional 4G LTE Cat 1, or 3G/2G variants that can be used for worldwide deployments, along with a 56-channel GPS receiver. The M8LZT also comes with BLE Bluetooth® connectivity, providing opportunities to connect and collect data from Bluetooth® devices and sensors.

Additional inputs and outputs also deliver enhanced monitoring capability, providing customers with deeper insights into their machines operating in the field beyond just data collection.

Connect

The telematics edge devices connect via a 4G cellular network for data transfer. When the machine is turned on, the telematics edge sends data immediately to Total Control®, after which event data is transmitted in real time, while sensor data is transmitted at configurable times, such as every 15 minutes. When the ignition is off, data is typically sent every hour.

Collect

The machine data is collected, filtered and normalized by ZTR's ONE i3™ back-office solution. Collected data is stored using many different technologies (SQL, NoSQL, flat file, etc.) in order to optimize the performance and data retention for all of the different data types and customer use cases. Through high performing APIs, data is inserted into the Total Control® service in near real time, providing UR and its customers with the latest information.

Data normalization occurs at the AWS gateway instance so data from different machines can be presented in a consistent way. For example, standard data formats are provided within the platform for different data types, such as analog values, discrete states or accumulators.

Aggregated data is generally stored for a fixed period of time in the live environment, after which the data is maintained in cold storage for longer periods and can be retrieved as necessary, for instance to support larger analytics projects.

Learn

Machines rented from UR, as well as customer-owned machines, can be viewed through the Total Control® interface. User activity is controlled by roles and permissions that determine what assets a user can see, what features a user can access, and what actions a user can perform.

Figure 15.4: UR Equipment on Rent with GPS

For instance, as shown in Fig. 15.4, customers can track what equipment is on rent.

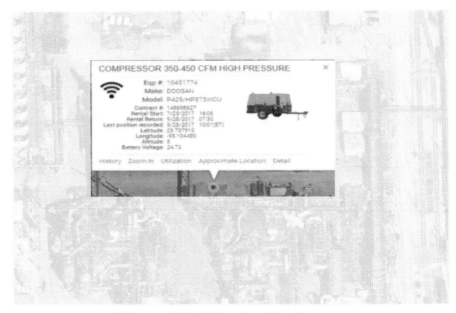

Figure 15.5: Mapping Equipment

Machine location is made visible, as shown in Fig. 15.5. Along with the ability to map comes the ability to track the machine's history, utilization, location and details about both the machine and rental transaction.

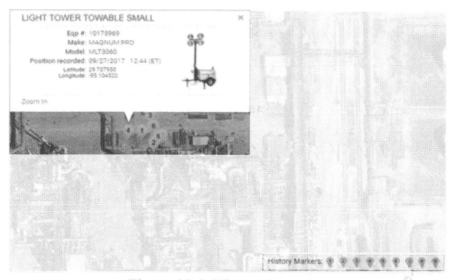

Figure 15.6: History Mapping

Total Control® also provides history mapping. This capability allows customers to see the equipment's last ten moves, displaying a marker that shows equipment make, model and number, along with position recorded by latitude and longitude.

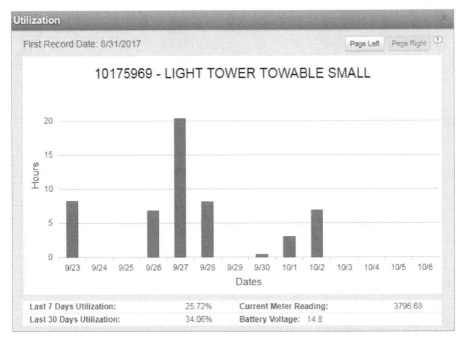

Figure 15.7: Utilization from Mapping

A core capability of Total Control® is utilization mapping. In figure 15.7, we see bars representing hours used per day, utilization for the last seven and last 30 days, and the current meter reading.

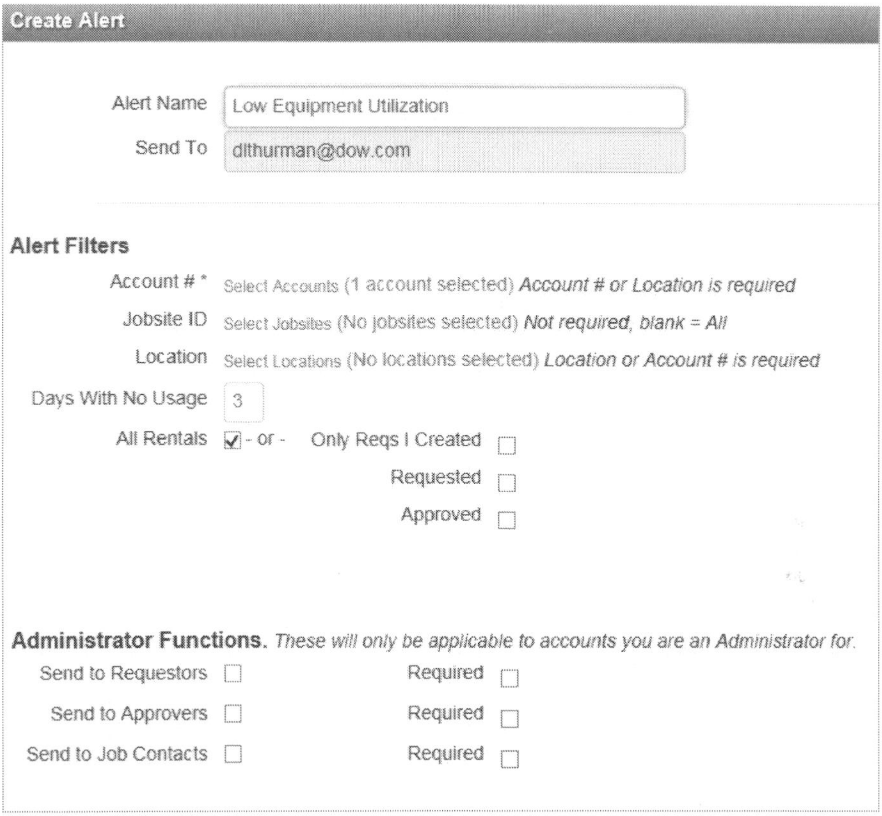

Alert Name | Low Equipment Utilization

Send To | dlthurman@dow.com

Alert Filters

Account # * | Select Accounts (1 account selected) *Account # or Location is required*

Jobsite ID | Select Jobsites (No jobsites selected) *Not required, blank = All*

Location | Select Locations (No locations selected) *Location or Account # is required*

Days With No Usage | 3

All Rentals ☑ - or - Only Reqs I Created ☐

Requested ☐

Approved ☐

Administrator Functions. *These will only be applicable to accounts you are an Administrator for.*

Send to Requestors ☐ | Required ☐

Send to Approvers ☐ | Required ☐

Send to Job Contacts ☐ | Required ☐

Figure 15.8: Consumption Management with Alerts

Customers can also set up an alert to notify them if a particular piece of equipment is idle for a specified amount of time. Multi-tier alerts can be set to notify various personnel that there is a lack of usage. Customers can also watch for pending and past-due alerts.

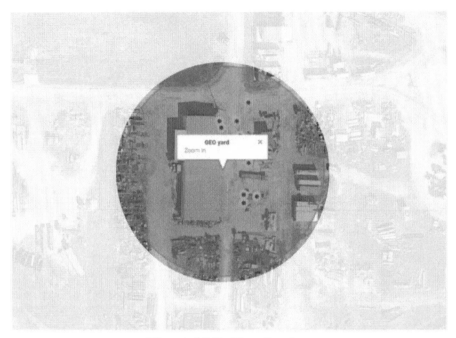

Figure 15.9: Geo-fencing

Geo-fencing is also available, providing alerts when equipment leaves and returns to a virtually-fenced area. One use case for geo-fencing is the creation of an auto-rental yard where equipment can be virtually checked out and back in by simply moving in and out of the virtually-fenced area; this capability is especially valued for secure job sites with heavily controlled access.

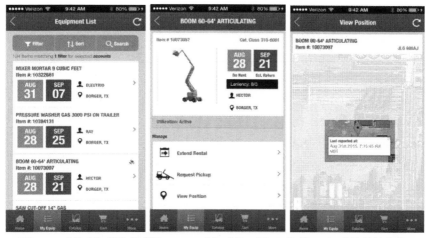

Figure 15.10: Visibility provided by Total Control® Mobile

Total Control® also provides a mobile app—available on both iOS and Android devices—to view and learn from the data being generated by the connected construction machines.

In summary, Total Control® offers a number of capabilities driven by telematics data that can help key stakeholders such as field foremen, purchasing agents and executives better manage construction projects. However, there is still the task of turning these potential benefits into reality.

Do

Connecting construction machines can enable construction companies to operate with greater precision. Gordon McDonald, vice president of managed services at United Rentals, has many great stories of how they improved the usage of machines and people on the construction site.

Getting Utilization Right

One of the best stories starts with Gordon demoing the Total Control® application for a major electrical contractor. During a meeting where Gordon was demonstrating the GPS capabilities in Total Control®, he noticed a $5,000/month excavator that hadn't moved in over two months. The contractor's CFO was shocked and immediately called the foreman on the job site. The foreman reported that the job had been delayed so the machine hadn't been used, but it was going to be used again "real soon." Both impressed and shocked by the findings, the CFO returned to the meeting and wanted to use the application himself. To everyone's surprise, the excavator no longer displayed. It turns out that immediately after the call, the foreman off-rented the excavator.

In addition, with Total Control®, customers cannot only identify the time of day equipment is being utilized, but also peak usage. Furthermore, the application can show if the utilization is below or above the benchmark across the entire UR fleet.

Using this data, one construction company reduced the number of scissor lifts they rented from ten to seven by rescheduling the work. Another company reduced the number of machines from 15 to seven. In both cases, not only did the customer reduce their overall rental costs but they also didn't have to pay for the additional operators.

Using this utilization information can be even more dramatic. For instance, Gordon has worked with a large entertainment company for more than ten years, and every time he'd visit the customer he couldn't help but notice that it seemed like a large number of the customer's owned equipment hadn't moved. One day, Gordon mentioned this to the gentleman in charge of maintenance.

Unfortunately, the customer had no visibility into the equipment's usage; therefore, Gordon had portable Slap Track devices put on about 300 of the customer's owned equipment and measured utilization over a period of about three months. It turns out the company was using its owned equipment with only about 10% utilization compared to the equipment rented from UR. As a result, the customer sold off 270 pieces of its own equipment.

Simple Utilization Data Not Enough
Sometimes we have to look deeper than simple utilization to uncover issues. Gordon shares a story where machines were indeed showing high rates of utilization. However, a closer look at the data showed that operators where spending a large percentage of their time traveling from location to location within the job site. An even deeper examination revealed that there was a location on the job site where people were often coming and spending 10–20 minutes, which looked like very short-duration work. In addition, there was a wide variety of equipment stopping at this particular location, but interestingly a vast majority was operator-run equipment like forklifts and backhoes. It turned out this location was being used as an informal smoking area. With this knowledge in hand, the job site foreman was able to address the matter.

At another job site the foreman told the operators they would lose the rental equipment if utilization was not high enough. The result was increased utilization, but it was because the operators were just turning on the machines and running them to increase the numbers. What the operators didn't realize was that Total Control® not only measures if equipment is running, but also if it's simply being kept idle.

Precision Billing

One challenge, especially at larger job sites, is distributing and assigning rental costs. Construction companies prefer a rental charge be not only charged to the job site, but also further broken down to a particular building or maintenance facility. Total Control® enables this through geo-fencing. With geo-fencing, when the customer gets a bill from UR, they're able to take that bill and distribute it across the different cost centers. The geo-fencing capability also enables "mod yards," which are commonly seen in Canada where building units are pre-assembled and taken to the site with minimal on-site construction required. In these cases, there are often several types of projects going on within a large area with equipment being rented full time but shared across the various projects. The customer wants to track where the rented equipment is being used so rental charges can be assigned based on usage by project.

Summary

Connected machines will also enable UR to provide new services as well as reduce their cost of maintaining a large fleet of construction machines through precision fueling. In the future, construction machines will send alerts when fuel is needed. This may help resolve an existing challenge on job sites, which is that machines can sometimes be missed when the fuel truck arrives. This can happen especially on larger sites where a piece of equipment might be in a remote area or hidden away somewhere. When a piece of equipment does run out of fuel, this can require a maintenance group to come out and bleed the injectors, etc. Therefore, by enabling the machines to notify the fuel supplier directly when fuel is needed, fuel drivers will be able to better verify that all equipment has been refueled prior to leaving a job site.

Total Control® also allows UR to set up maintenance schedules for its own equipment and that of its customers based on real-time equipment utilization data. UR can tell customers that they have equipment due for maintenance in the next X number of run hours or Y number of days. This drives efficiencies for the mechanics because when they're in a specific area to work on currently due machines, they can also check out the machines that are near due. Before Total Control®, personnel would have to be physically sent to inspect the hours on equipment to know if maintenance was due. In the future, machines will be able to schedule service on demand versus on a scheduled basis, not only improving machine availability, but also reducing the overall cost.

And this is just the beginning. You can be sure that Mike Bierschbach, Sam Hassan, Gordon McDonald and their teams will be continuing to transform vision into reality so that someday, precision construction is just the way we do business.

16

Precision Solar Energy Project

In 2017, a large power company announced the winning contractor to run a solar energy project with a total capacity of approximately 300 MW. This was part of an extensive renewable energy program designed to provide enough electricity to serve about 100,000 homes with clean power. With capital costs estimated at less than $1,500/kW, these would be among the lowest cost solar installations built in the United States. In support of this contract, the awarded contractor rented machines from United Rentals.

This story actually begins with frustrations borne from an old process. Previously, the awarded contractor's procurement team was driving all of the rentals, meaning UR had to provide a new quote every time the customer needed any piece of equipment, from skid steers to bucket attachments. This was exhausting, cumbersome and time consuming for UR and the customer alike.

Recognizing the inefficiencies, Shawna Ermold, the national account manager from UR managing the contractor account, decided to jumpstart a different kind of conversation. This new conversation focused on utilization measured through Key Performance Indicators (KPIs) based on data driven through UR Total Control® and UR's Tool Solutions' mobile tool room.

In a nutshell, Shawna held regular KPI meetings with the customer where she and her team identified underutilized rented assets based on parameters set up ahead of time. They would then coach the customer on how to better manage these underutilized assets to help them improve their return on rental investment.

At the end of this, the relationship evolved from being one focused on bidding out all the time to one where UR was invited to consult on opportunities for the customer to improve its operations. Of course, at the heart of enabling this program was access to the data.

Things

A variety of machines were rented by this contractor to complete the solar energy project, including equipment such as skid steers and utility vehicles. Data was retrieved from all machines using Total Control®, UR's telematics-enabled fleet- and equipment-management system that provides visibility into both rented and owned equipment with an objective of improving utilization, maintenance and uptime.

United Rentals also provided its mobile tool room to the contractor. This is a semi-truck stocked with tools and supplies for a customer's project. The contractor used well over one hundred different types of tools, everything from ladders to impact wrenches and laser levels to crimpers. The mobile tool room was delivered directly to the power company's sites and was managed by a UR tools expert who checked out tools to authorized users, while also providing maintenance services and safety oversight. The goal of UR's Tool Solutions is to create the most uptime or 'wrench time' for its customers, effectively increasing productivity. There are estimates that 20% of a construction worker's day is spent looking for, waiting for, or fixing tools and equipment.

A focus of Shawna's program for the contractor was to provide visibility into rental utilization. For tools, the benchmark goal was roughly 85% utilization, which meant keeping 85% of the active tools in the mobile tool room utilized 100% of the time. To determine tool utilization, there's an assumption that if the tool is not in the onsite mobile tool room, it's being used.

On the other hand, various pieces of general-rental equipment are used differently and therefore are assigned different utilization benchmark goals. For example, the customer had a benchmark goal for utility vehicles of 22% time utilization across all job sites. Whereas for skid steers, the utilization goal in some cases was set at 200% of the industry norm because of the type of work being performed.

Connect

All machines had telematics edge devices installed for the retrieval of data from the field. Older rental machines were retrofitted with a device sourced from ZTR that provided run hours, location, battery level, fuel level, driver ID and external conditions. Newer machines that came telematics-enabled from the manufacturers had a custom ZTR device installed. This device provided the same data as the retrofit use case, plus equipment monitoring data such as error codes. Finally, for temporary situations, a portable "Slap Track" device was installed to provide machine location and an estimate of run hours based on vibrations.

As for tools, a bar code system was used to check tools in and out to a specific person, who then had accountability for that asset. Data was stored in Total Control® for managing and tracking tooling, bulk items and consumables that are being managed through the mobile tool room.

Collect

Collected machine data is communicated to Total Control®'s backend systems running on AWS. Data is stored using many different technologies (SQL, NoSQL, flat file, etc.) in order to optimize the performance and data retention for all of the different customer use cases. Time-series data targets operational needs by providing current values, recent history and real-time events for fleet tracking, equipment health management and system integrations. Aggregated data drives reports and business intelligence that Shawna and her peers used to support analysis for fleet optimization, contract management, etc. Aggregated data is generally stored for 13 months, after which the data is maintained in cold storage for longer periods and can be retrieved for other needs, such as larger analytics projects.

Learn

By connecting the machine and the customer, Shawna was able to use data collected by Total Control® to learn how UR could deliver a higher quality service to the contractor, as well as save them money. The four key metrics, or KPIs, they focused on were: on-time delivery, service calls, exchanges and machine utilization.

	Week 1	Week 2	Week 3	Week 4	Week 5	Week 6
D: < 24 Hours Notice	13	22	7	12	5	12
C: < 48 Hours Notice	3	11	2	8	4	9
B: < 72 Hours Notice	3	4	5	6	4	1
A: > 72 Hours Notice	27	51	34	41	29	18

	Week 1	Week 2	Week 3	Week 4	Week 5	Week 6
Delivered On Time	45	84	40	65	39	38
Delivered Late	1	4	8	2	3	2

Figure 16.1: On time Delivery Example
(Customer actual data changed for privacy reasons)

KPI: Lead Time and Delivery Performance
UR started off with measuring and reporting on-time delivery performance. This was important for two reasons. First, UR gave the contractor an on-time delivery guarantee for orders placed with a minimum of 72-hours' notice, so they needed to track if they were delivering equipment on time per this guarantee. But also, UR wanted to know if failure to deliver equipment on time was due to short lead-time requests by the customer.

Shawna used Total Control® to analyze data for the percentage of orders made in four categories: less than 24-hours' notice, less than 48-hours' notice, less than 72-hours' notice, and greater than 72-hours' notice.

As shown Fig.16.1, UR reported not only on its ability to deliver on time, but it also mapped this to the amount of notice. This transparency with the customer held UR accountable for on-time deliveries while also showing the contractor how late-notice orders impacted the on-time delivery of the machines.

KPI: Service Calls
Service calls were also measured. Service calls included events such as engine issues, air conditioning not working and tire problems. One common service call was repair requests for air conditioners. This isn't too surprising considering the weather at the sites was over 100+ degree heat and 90% humidity.

Upon further investigation, it was discovered that many of the repair requests for air conditioners came from cabbed equipment that were being used by workers solely for the purpose of cooling down. The high utilization data from the running vehicles along with the common issue of broken A/C units on those vehicles provided an opportunity for the contractor to better manage its process for helping employees deal with the elements while also avoiding unnecessary equipment service costs.

	Month 1	Month 2	Month 3	Month 4	Month 5
Customer Service Call - Equipment Failure	3	1	4	18	3
Wrong Equipment Number	2	3	4	2	
Equipment Unsuitable for Job	3	1	2	3	1
Needed for Rental or Sale				2	1
Equipment Failed During Checkout	1			2	
Exchange from Rerent		1	1	1	
Equipment to be Serviced				1	

Figure 16.2: Equipment Exchanges Example
(Customer actual data changed for privacy reasons)

KPI: Equipment Exchanges
Equipment exchange data was also collected. As shown in Fig. 16.2, the data showed an abnormally high level of exchanges in Month 4. After the team investigated why and the root cause was determined, UR and the customer worked together to identify equipment better suited to the customer's needs.

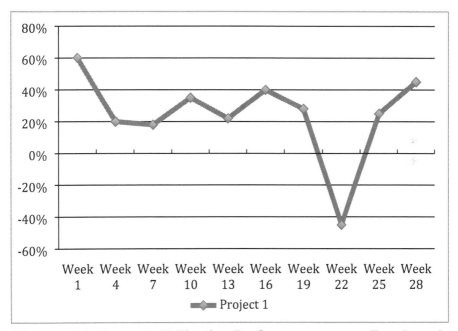

Figure 16.3: Example Utilization Performance versus Benchmark
(Customer actual data changed for privacy reasons)

KPI: Utilization Performance vs. Benchmark

Finally, the most important metric was utilization against agreed upon benchmark performance objectives. As a company that collects nearly 10 million lines of data per week, UR is able to calculate statistically reliable benchmarks by industry and application, ultimately providing the customer with unique insights into how they perform against an anonymous peer set.

Utilization performance means actual hours used versus hours rented, while the benchmark represents an industry utilization benchmark. An example snapshot of this report is shown in Fig. 16.3, where 0% reflects that actual utilization is at the benchmark value. To further elaborate, if the utilization data is above 0%, say at 20%, then this means utilization is 20% above the benchmark. Likewise, if utilization is below the 0% line, say at -60%, this means utilization is 60% below the established benchmark.

The significant dip in utilization that occurred around week 22 shown in Fig. 16.3 was a result of a temporary change in project management. Once this was identified to the customer, they were able to take steps to remedy the situation.

One of the reasons why the customer's utilization was mostly good is that alerts were set up in Total Control® to send automated emails if a machine had sat underutilized for three days. This notified the contractor to investigate those machines and enabled them to decide whether to off-rent the underutilized equipment or start using them more.

Do

In the end, UR helped the contractor save over 12% on its rental costs for an approximate $7 million project. But it's not only a story about saving money. It's also a story about UR helping the customer by using data and insights to deliver better service.

Weekly reports went out to the contractor's executive staff and project managers that provided the customer with visibility—mid-month or mid-bill cycle—into fuel discussions. With a common view of the data, in the meetings, the UR team discussed service issues, utilization, exchanges and upcoming rentals. They also talked about the opportunities to off-rent various machines based on their overall utilization for the last month. Project managers used the data from Total Control® to see outliers in the data and then investigate those on site in order to make better utilization decisions. Essentially, Shawna and the customer focused on the issues rather than on what was going well, something Shawna calls 'management by exception.'

In the end, the relationship evolved from being transactional to one where UR was invited to consult on opportunities for the customer to improve its operations. Of course, at the heart of enabling this program was access to the data.

17

Precision Contractor

When you live in Silicon Valley you tend to think startups were born there, but of course, that's not true. Less than a decade after the end of WWII, a man between jobs was looking for construction work with the help of his community, which led to his getting hired to remove the lath and plaster from the walls and ceiling of a local trustee building. At the same time, his friend was finishing up a small job, so they decided to do the lath and plaster together, assuming they'd split ways after the work was over. But as you can guess, the friends didn't split ways and instead continued working together, giving start to one of the largest construction companies today.

This Precision Contractor is part of a larger group that generates more than $1 billion per year in revenue among all its companies and has done a number of major projects, including building multi-million-dollar bridges, dirt and rock excavating, laying gas and water pipelines, and building several water and waste treatment plants in the U.S.

One long-standing employee, Tim, while he hasn't been there since the beginning, has worked for this contractor for over 25 years. From his vantage point of leading the company's telematics program and working with the AEMP (Association of Equipment Management Professionals), Tim can see firsthand how contractors are being squeezed between end customers wanting lower costs and construction equipment becoming more expensive as technology continues to evolve. In addition, labor is becoming less available and therefore more expensive, but is also relatively untrained. As a result, Tim sees a clear mandate: increase the productivity of the equipment and labor used on construction projects in order to lower overall construction costs.

He also sees the need to further enhance both security and safety at the job site. No one wants an expensive piece of equipment to be stolen, and no one wants someone without the right training and privileges to start a machine and potentially get hurt. But before any of this could be accomplished, the machines needed to be connected.

Things

The Precision Contractor's equipment division has a trained staff of over 200 personnel and services more than 1,300 company-owned, large equipment pieces. They have implemented a support system that provides equipment and supplies on site when needed.

In the early 2000s, the company had the foresight to build a custom hardware and software system to provide data from the construction machines used in the field. They decided to engineer their own system because, at the time, no one offered an off-the-shelf solution that provided telematics data (e.g., hours, location) along with fuel consumption.

To engineer this connected system, the company partnered with a local embedded systems company, and as is the case with many stories, it turns out the owners of the two companies were old friends; the rest, as they say, is history.

The system currently monitors up to four discrete switches and two analog sensors. These vary by machine based on the application and what the company is monitoring and measuring. For instance, one machine may monitor a load/bed switch while another monitors forward and reverse motion. The system can also read any J1939 data provided on the machine.

Connect

In 2008, the cost of a cellular connection was $30–$50 per month, so connecting many hundreds of machines was very expensive. As a result, this contractor made the decision to make the fuel-control panel act as the hub for the network. The fuel-control panel is connected to the Precision Contractor's servers by WiFi or cellular. All of the construction machines are then Zigbee connected to the fuel-control panels.

In operation, the fuel trucks pull up to the equipment and the fuel-truck operator logs into the fuel panel, puts the hose into the machine and pushes a button near the fuel cap. At that point data is transmitted up to the servers. Today, about 50 fuel trucks support around 800 connected machines.

In addition to the fuel-control panel, a secondary data-collector panel can also be deployed, which typically is mounted on a manager's truck. It serves the same purpose of providing a link back to headquarters. And whereas the fuel-control panel only provides connectivity when the fuel truck is within range, the data-collector panel stays on site, which is especially important for transferring more critical operations data in real time. That said, non-critical data is transferred about every twenty minutes from the panels.

Collect

All data is sent to the Precision Contractor's datacenter and raw data is initially stored in a Microsoft SQL server database. The data is scrubbed once per day and then stored directly into a Viewpoint Vista ERP system. Logs are indexed to the individual machine level. This includes hour-meter data and idle time. Employees can access data through an application that provides access to data sitting in the ERP database. They archive on a rolling 12-month period but have data from the beginning of the project, approaching nearly a decade.

Service management and trouble ticketing is also handled through Viewpoint. In general, the field problems are written down in a problem log. On-site planners, who take care of parts ordering and location transfers, also enter their information.

Learn

The application only lets you see jobs in your area if you're an area manager, while an executive has full access. The top five outliers are shown by idle time, operator and job, and from there you can drill into information about the different machines' utilization. While we were on the phone with Tim, he got a message that an operator had reported a bent bar on one of the machines. Tim then ran a report to see the last three people who used the machine.

Managing utilization of operators and equipment is a big part of a construction project's cost, but it's not just reports that matter; there also needs to be the human element. For example, sometimes 40% idle time is acceptable, as you might have a load on a boom lift that is holding some piece in place. The engine isn't on, but the machine is clearly being utilized.

Do

Tim is quick to point out that previously, the Precision Contractor was still attempting to gather much of the same information that the connected machines are providing today, such as hour meters and fuel usage. The key difference is that before, this was all done through a manual process, which introduced time delays, human errors and labor costs into the process—ironically, deterrents to enhancing productivity.

Now, with data generated from machines in the field loading directly into ERP systems, customers can track, drive and verify things like cost recording with fuel-usage data, preventative-maintenance schedules with hour meters, and billed-hour confirmation against actual machine usage.

A big challenge for customers like this is that the same physical key can start all equipment from a particular manufacturer. As an example, a particular John Deere key will start up *any* piece of John Deere equipment within a certain year range, regardless of which company owns the unit. This is the same with CAT, Komatsu and many others. Tim still has the original CAT keys he was first issued 25 years ago, but they still work on two-thirds of the CAT equipment in their fleet. This creates the vulnerability that very expensive equipment can more easily be stolen.

Tim shares a story from a time before their machines were connected, when a disgruntled ex-employee stole an excavator from a job in the hills of Kentucky, driving the $300,000 piece of equipment up a mountaintop and down the other side, where he promptly set it on fire.

Using traditional keys to start equipment also means there are no safeguards in place as to who can start up and run a piece of equipment, which introduces safety risks as well. For instance, if a group of kids were to happen upon a construction site and find a key that enabled them to start equipment, it could be a very tragic day if someone got hurt.

In an attempt to solve these challenges, machine manufacturers tried to put keypads on their equipment with a programmable, company specific code. However, this approach failed fairly quickly once everyone knew the code, as codes were not tied to specific operators.

In response, this Precision Contractor gave Honeywell HID security cards to operators and added readers to equipment that tied to the specific machines. Cards are assigned to individual, active employees. This not only limits the ability for just any employee to start and run any machine, but it also prevents theft, as ex-employee access privileges can be immediately terminated.

Tim gives the example of when there was an obvious attempted theft of a Bobcat skid-steer loader. When the thieves tried to start it but couldn't, they got frustrated and beat up the dashboard. But in the end, having a connected machine stopped a $70,000 asset from being stolen. In the old days, the company might lose two to three skid-steer-size machines per year. In fact, they once had a Caterpillar D5 bulldozer stolen out of the median strip of a highway. Today, stories like these are in the rear-view mirror.

On the back-office side, the company has the ability to tie the completion of training to an operator's security card so only those with the proper training and credentials for that specific model of machine are able to start it. All of this prevents a random person with the right key to hop in a cabin and turn the ignition on.

Connecting the machine and the operator also allows for operator-performance tracking. Now, because it is known precisely *who* started up and ran a particular piece of equipment, usage can be tied directly back to the operator. Companies can track individual operator run and idle time, thus individual performance, versus only knowing machine utilization regardless of who actually ran the equipment. Without connectivity, companies have to manually match up time cards or payroll entries with equipment usage.

Tracking operator performance is much less about a contractor playing the role of Big Brother, and more about reducing idle time by better coaching its operators. For example, by looking at an operator's idle-time performance over, say, five different machines, a company can know how well he does at managing his utilization. And if he does a poor job, the company is able to help him improve through coaching.

Finally, HID cards also help in addressing the issue of equipment damage that often goes unreported. Now, a company can narrow the list of potential suspects by knowing who started the machine during the period of time when the machine was damaged. Tim says he has a lot of examples with basically the same storyline. He gets a call from a mechanic or a superintendent in the field saying, "Hey, can you run the report and tell me who started all my trucks over the last week? Because I have some damage on a piece of equipment and no one is owning up to it." So, the company can run the report and boil it down to a few people, enabling them to figure out the culprit from there.

Summary

In Tim's opinion, companies are at different levels of sophistication when it comes to equipment management, meaning not everyone views equipment management the same way. For this Precision Contractor, equipment management enabled through connected construction machines is a competitive advantage.

Tim also believes people just expect that IoT will give them insights that maybe they wouldn't have had before. He shares that his company takes a slightly different approach, saying, "First we figure out what we want to improve on and that will tell us what we need to measure, which will tell us what data we need to collect from the machines." In other words, don't look at what a connection can do, but instead, figure out the business case you're trying to improve upon and then work backwards.

So, what's next? The Precision Contractor is starting to explore automatic location transfer of the machines based on their GPS information, as well as use the ISO 15143 standard for earth-moving machinery. In 2016, ISO approved the new mixed-fleet standard, which enables machine users to gather more machine data into their preferred business- or fleet-management software. ISO 15143-3:2016 further specifies the communication schema designed to provide machine-status data from a manufacturer's server to a third-party client application via the internet. This standard describes the communication records used to request data from the server, and the responses from the server containing specified data elements to be used in the analysis of machine performance and health.

Tim started on this journey with his company eight years ago primarily to manage fuel costs; at $3 or $4 per gallon, it can be a large part of a construction project's costs. Now with data, they even enjoy a competitive advantage in the bidding process. While there will clearly be more and more data for them to analyze, Tim reminds us that sometimes it's the simple things that matter.

18

Precision Scissor and Boom Lifts

Guru Bandekar is Vice President of Global Engineering and Program Management at JLG Industries. JLG was founded in 1969 and today is a 3+ billion-dollar corporation. It is a leading designer and manufacturer of boom lifts, scissor lifts, telehandlers and stock pickers.

Guru sees the pressure—and opportunity—that JLG faces in an increasingly commoditized world. In response, JLG is embedding more electronics into equipment and hiring more software developers and data scientists to further differentiate its products. This creates the opportunity for JLG to better meet the needs of both end customers and rental companies to enhance productivity by connecting their machines.

Things

Figure 18.1: JLG Boom Lift and Scissor Lift

A scissor lift is a type of platform that typically moves vertically and is used to elevate workers to high areas on a job site. Scissor lifts are good for jobs that need to elevate multiple workers, as the size of the platform tends to be much larger than with other types of aerial lifts.

The mechanism in place that enables vertical movement is a linked, folding support in a scissor-like "X" pattern, hence the name. The contraction of the scissor action can be hydraulic, pneumatic or mechanical (via a leadscrew or rack and pinion system). Depending on the lift's power system, it may require no power to enter descent mode, but rather a simple release of hydraulic or pneumatic pressure. This is the main reason that these methods of powering the lifts are preferred, as it allows a fail-safe option of returning the platform to the ground by release of a manual valve.

A boom lift is a type of aerial lift that supports a hydraulic arm that is capable of maneuvering around obstacles. There are two basic types of boom lifts: articulating and telescopic. Articulating boom lifts have arms that bend, making it easier to move the bucket around objects. Telescopic boom lifts have straight arms and usually higher weight capacities, but are more difficult to maneuver.

Boom lifts can extend much higher than scissor lifts. Whereas scissor lifts typically reach heights of 20–50 feet, boom lifts can extend up to 185 feet. Also, because most scissor lifts only move vertically, there is no way to maneuver them up and around obstacles. Boom lifts tend to be more expensive, with a weekly rental price that's often more than twice that of its scissor-lift counterpart.

Figure 18.2: JLG Standard Four-Pin Telematics-Ready Plug

JLG connected its full line of scissor and boom lifts using ORBCOMM software and hardware.

JLG's 19-foot scissor lift is connected using the ORBCOMM 3-wire ClearSky Locate device, which plugs into JLG's four-pin plug (shown in Fig. 18.2), and measures location, on/off and battery level.

JLG's 40-, 60- and 80-foot boom lifts make up over 80% of the total market. As a leader in these categories, JLG machines are connected with an ORBCOMM PT7000 device that interfaces with the machine's CAN bus. It includes sensors to measure location, on/off, battery level, duty cycle, load type, engine speed, RPM, fault codes, engine or idol hours, fuel consumption, battery voltage and geo-fencing. The ORBCOMM PT7000 has four digital inputs, two digital outputs and four analog inputs. It supports both J1939 and J1798 protocols, meaning it can support multiple CAN buses. It's powered by the machine but also has a 9-volt backup battery.

Connect

Both the scissors and booms connect using 3G cellular, Bluetooth® or WiFi, and can also connect via satellite for use in remote areas or mines. The software in the ORBCOMM box can be updated remotely over the air via cellular or satellite.

Once the machine is connected, it can be configured or reconfigured depending on what JLG wants to do with it and the type of data they want to pull off the machine. The device is set to pull machine data every two to three minutes, and those data transmissions are typically 5–6 kilobytes in size.

Collect

Data coming off JLG's machines is initially collected at different clouds depending on the use case. JLG offers its own ClearSky platform for customers to manage their fleets of JLG equipment. ClearSky runs on AWS. In some cases data is collected at the customer's cloud via an API. In other cases, data first goes to ORBCOMM's FleetEdge platform, which runs on a third-party private cloud in its tier-two data center in Virginia. Data is privately archived in short-term storage for about six months, at which point it's moved to a long-term archive.

Figure 18.3: ClearSky Dashboard

IT service and parts management data are collected in a customized ERP application, which also has deep integration with JLG's custom-built warranty management application called Service Bench. In addition, add*ONE is used as the parts forecasting tool. Finally, JLG collects call-handling data using a Cisco system.

Learn

For ClearSky customers, once a machine has been associated with a serial number, it's provisioned or allocated to a customer's ClearSky account. This means that once customers log into the application, they are able to see and view machines in their fleet, as shown in Fig. 18.3. At a high level they can view where a machine is located, or they can dive deeper into any number of machines in their fleet to view more detailed information, such as tire pressure or the angle of the boom, depending on the type or class of machine.

To access JLG's ClearSky, a customer uses industry standard login/password authentication. JLG requires all customer-facing sites, even ones with no sign in, to be secured using HTTPS.

Once logged in, the customer gains access to information depending on his or her privileges. For example, a full fleet manager might be given access to all machines within a particular customer's fleet, while a branch manager may only be granted privileges to view a subset of machines in the fleet, and a mechanic might only have access to a specific machine. Access control is structured as a hierarchy from the customer perspective, with a high-level admin having access to all machine data. Then sub admins are assigned narrower views of the data. JLG acts as an admin in creating these customer accounts.

Do

Analysis of data helps JLG, the rental company and the customer to understand true utilization—both optimal and actual—of the machines in the field. Optimal utilization includes, for instance, reporting if a machine is being run out of spec, over speed, beyond a tilt angle, or being operated in an unsafe manner. On the other hand, actual utilization reports if a machine is sitting idle at a job site or is being transported—indicated by full-wheel-drive activity moving through a site and over certain distances.

Many of JLG's biggest customers are rental companies, so if a machine can't be rented, it's a loss for the company; therefore, predictive maintenance reports are a big deal. Utilizing data for predictive maintenance not only means telling the customer that, based on usage, it's time to change the equipment's oil, but it also means the ability to predict potential future errors depending on error codes across the customer's entire fleet of JLG equipment. Today with ClearSky, you can see when the last maintenance was performed as well as the next scheduled maintenance. In the future, JLG hopes to use the sensor data to recommend service based on actual utilization and the performance of a specific boom or scissor lift.

JLG also uses data to understand total cost of ownership. For any particular machine, JLG knows what type of duty cycle a machine is operated on and what kind of use and abuse it suffered. Therefore, based on the type of maintenance required, the age of the machine, the cost of the machine, the types of replacement parts a customer has purchased, the cost of operations of a given machine and relative values compared to the rest of their fleet, JLG can determine how much the machine costs to stay up and running. This overall picture reveals if it's worth it financially to keep up a particular machine or sell it and buy a new one. JLG also uses this information to send recommendations back to the rental agencies as to when a machine is no longer cost effective to maintain.

Most of JLG's revenue today is a combination of selling new machines and parts for their installed base, but they are beginning to provide some new services for a select group of customers. For example, for an annual fee per machine, JLG will monitor the machines and make service recommendations. Another service provides a continuous connection to their parts-management system, and if the customer commits to using only JLG parts, the parts will be delivered quickly and at a discount to the retail price.

Summary

Guru says the last two years have been about connecting the machines. In the next two years, a connected machine will be the norm and the conversation will shift to who owns the data and what value can be created by it. Does the machine manufacturer own the data? Does the rental company own the data? Or does the user of the machine own the data? And what data are we talking about? Is it the sensor data, the warranty claims, the last service call or the last part ordered?

And if you look another few years into the future, the electrification wave that has begun to hit the automobile market will surely change boom and scissor lifts. Today, the drive trains on these machines are diesel powered, but diesel engines not only require a lot of care and feeding, but they are also noisy; so it seems a safe bet that many of these drive trains will be changed to electric motors. The lifts themselves are another matter. For smaller lifts it's likely they will not be hydraulic, but also move to electric. For the larger lifts however, hydraulics are probably here to stay.

As with cars, the machines will get smarter and smarter. SAE International standard J3016 defines six levels of automation for automakers, suppliers and policymakers to classify a system's sophistication. Today's scissor and boom lifts operate with around 10,000 lines of code, but with the addition of more sensors and more compute power, these lifts will become much smarter. It's possible they will reach level 3 (conditional automation) or level 4 (high automation) for some of the repetitive jobs.

But will all of this result in lifting as a service? In the world of cars, we're already seeing rides as a service, which when combined with autonomy has the potential to disrupt the automobile industry. Of course, that's when it's easy to move the machine around. It might be a while before we see an autonomous boom lift moving from construction site to construction site, but you can rest assured that whatever the future holds, Guru and JLG will be a part of it.

19

Precision Track Loaders

Chris Hulsey works at TALISMAN Rentals, an Atlanta-based construction equipment rental company and division of the TALISMAN Hire Group. He has been in the business for more than 10 years and has seen it all, but technology is helping him to see even more.

One Monday morning, a Georgia-based customer who had rented a Takeuchi excavator for a week, returned the equipment claiming he shouldn't be charged for the rental because he hadn't used it. Unfortunately for the customer, Chris checked the status of the machine on his Takeuchi Fleet Management portal to find that the customer had not only used the piece of equipment but had also taken the machine all the way down to Florida. Chris told the customer: "I can see that you started the machine every day at 5 a.m. and ran it until 2 p.m. I suspect you must have taken a lunch break because you refueled and fired the equipment back up at 3 p.m." The customer was caught in his lie and simply responded, "Yeah, you got me."

This devious customer thought he could pull one over on the rental company because, as Chris puts it, TALISMAN seems like a "small, mom and pop store." But in reality, the customer was dealing with a premium rental agency with access to the latest in telematics technology. As Chris says: "We only buy industrial strength, quality equipment that we know can last, requires the least amount of maintenance, and can be managed the most effectively […] and this means if [a machine] doesn't have telematics, we're not going to buy it." Included on the list of construction machines Chris buys and rents are excavators and track loaders from Takeuchi.

Things

Takeuchi developed the world's first compact excavator in 1970 and in the mid-80's introduced the first compact track loader. Today, Takeuchi builds a line of seven compact excavators and five track loader models.

Figure 19.1: TL12V2 Track Loader

This story focuses on the Takeuchi TL12V2 track loader. A tracked loader is a machine consisting of a tracked (not wheeled) chassis with a loader for digging and loading material. The ability of a track loader to perform almost every task on a job site is why it is part of many companies' fleets.

Figure 19.2: ZTR M8HZT

All TL12V2s are equipped with TFM. At the machine level, TFM is implemented with ZTR Control Systems' M8HZT telematics device, (shown in Fig. 19.2) providing data to ZTR's ONE i3™ back-office solution that powers the TFM application. Takeuchi installs the M8HZT in its factory as part of the manufacturing process. Data is gathered from the control units by a connection to the equipment's CAN bus network, as all onboard sensors and controllers feed into it. TFM-enabled Takeuchi machines provide a range of sensor-based information, including engine torque, injector metering rail pressure, hydraulic oil temperature, machine location, engine speed, battery voltage, engine oil pressure, engine coolant temperature, fuel level, fuel consumption rate, DPF (diesel particulate filter) status, trip meters and last communication. In addition, standard J1939 fault codes as well as Takeuchi-specific fault codes are provided.

The M8HZT, which reports this sensor data, is powered by the machine's 12-volt battery, with backup power provided by a 5200mAH lithium ion rechargeable battery.

Connect

The M8HZT connects across a 4G cellular network operating over LTE Cat 1 700, 850, 1900 and 2100 MHz frequency bands. The solution can also be provided with 3G and 2G coverage for worldwide operations, which is important for an OEM that is supplying machines globally. The wireless carrier provides a private APN/VPN so all data is protected during transmission. GPS location is provided over satellite through a 56-channel GPS, using a satellite-based augmentation system (SBAS). When the equipment is turned on, the machine sends data immediately to the Takeuchi Fleet Management application. From that point on, data is transmitted every 15 minutes, and when the ignition is turned off, data is sent every hour.

Collect

Data is collected, filtered and normalized by ZTR's ONE i3™ back-office solution, which in turn powers Takeuchi's TFM solution. Takeuchi also pulls the data once per day through a custom API call to feed other key business systems. The data is then stored in a Microsoft SQL server database located at Takeuchi's data center where it's archived for 18 months. To date, Takeuchi has collected about 50GB of information.

Takeuchi collects warranty claim requests using PTC's iWarranty application. Each regional service manager has a queue where they will see new pending claims, parts returned for inspection, and claims in a current parts-return status. They will review and approve the claims, but final approval is made at the national level. They also use iWarranty for machine registration and service bulletin assignments. For product service and support, the current systems are based on ShoreTel call management and email.

Learn

The TFM application, powered by ZTR's ONE i3™ includes modules for mapping, assets, alerts, maintenance planning and analytics. This gives users of Takeuchi machines access to data such as location, utilization, performance and maintenance. It also gives any user insights into where and how the equipment is being operated.

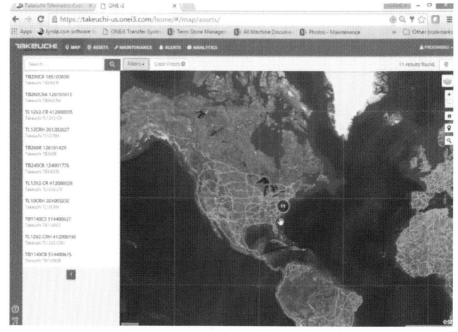

Figure 19.3: TFM user interface–map

Machine failure is almost always related to machine operations, such as the operator running a machine with an active error code. For example, when an engine begins to overheat it will initially result in an audible alarm, flashing caution light and an active error code present on the machine's display. As the machine continues to be operated while overheating, the active error codes, engine temperatures, run time and other useful diagnostic information is being stored in TFM. Operators will often just turn the machine off and restart, which will clear the code; but the machine will continue to overheat, which will inevitably result in engine damage. Expensive repairs are avoidable if the operator shuts the machine down after the first alarm and repairs or finds the cause of the overheating, such as low coolant or a dirty radiator. In the days before machines were connected, the operator might have gone back to the dealer with a damaged machine, which would have to be covered under the two-year warranty period. Today, in the connected state, Takeuchi can more fully evaluate the circumstances of a failure when judged against the warranty, for example, if data shows the operator ran the machine properly or ignored error codes.

Takeuchi can also use data to help operators learn how to better operate their machines. For example, the conventional wisdom for operating diesel engines is to let them idle (i.e., don't ever shut them down). While that might have been true in the past, idling Tier IV, DPF-equipped diesel engines is one of the worst things one can do, as they don't burn as clean or as hot at idle. This can result in a prematurely clogged diesel particulate filter. The problem with this is the machine will either require more frequent regeneration or go into a state where the DPF will need to be removed and professionally cleaned. Regeneration will also be required more frequently if operators run their diesel engines with an average load rate of only 20% or less.

Regeneration is associated with diesel engines equipped with a DPF, which is a device designed to remove diesel particulate matter or soot from the exhaust gas of a diesel engine. As the filter becomes clogged it becomes restrictive and needs to be cleaned using a process called regeneration to "burn off" carbon particles in the exhaust filter. Most often, the regeneration occurs automatically during normal operation without the operator even knowing. However, in some instances, the machine may require a parked regeneration, which requires the machine to be stationary while it completes a thorough cleaning (regeneration) to restore the effectiveness of the exhaust filter. Regeneration can last 30–45 minutes—all unproductive downtime.

Takeuchi machines have five alarm levels with regard to regeneration. At levels 1 and 2 there is a beep every 10 seconds, followed by the regeneration light illuminated on the operator's console. At level 3 there is a beep every second and an active error code, which requests the operator to stop the machine and do a regeneration. When level 4 is reached, the dealer has to come out to the field and force regeneration by connecting a laptop to the machine. And when a machine reaches level 5, it's time to take the filter off and get it professionally cleaned. In any case, ignoring alerts can result in costly repairs.

With access to machine data through TFM, dealers gain visibility into machines that are idling too long and therefore at risk of needing more frequent regeneration. For instance, when these machines were used in colder climates, such as working on oil field locations in Northern Canada, a standard practice was to idle the engine all night to eliminate the possibility of the machine not starting the next morning due to cold weather. During the night the audible alarms would be ignored, and the machine would be in a de-rated level 5 soot load status the next morning. Now with TFM, dealers and Takeuchi can recommend that the machines be shut down at night and kept warm with a block heater, as they can monitor the machine's precise status.

In terms of maintenance, Takeuchi recommends a 500-hour service interval in most machines. Using machine data captured by TFM, it's known when a machine is coming up on this service interval. This allows the dealership time to get prepared with the right parts in stock for the customer's model, as well as to reach out to the customer to schedule the service appointment. Before TFM, machines were often run to a point where they needed to be immediately stopped to perform particular procedures. Now with data, maintenance can be scheduled for when a machine will not be needed on a job with customizable, proactive alerts.

Do

Before Takeuchi machines were connected they may see a failure of some sort about six times a year. These failures were due to several things, such as dirty air filters, dead batteries and operator misuse. Now, with connected machines, there are significant improvements to machine availability. For Chris, this means he has the information he needs to stay on top of maintenance, saying, "If I can keep my equipment maintained, it will keep running so the customer gets the job done on time and doesn't go over budget."

With the ability to diagnose a connected machine, Chris can save the end customer from a hefty bill to have a tech come on site. Customers can call in and say that a machine is beeping and they don't know what to do. With TFM, TALISMAN Rentals can see, for instance, that the machine just needs a regeneration, allowing them to walk the customer through that procedure. If they have to roll a truck to the machine, the customer is looking at a $500–$1,000 charge.

Connecting machines also allows for new business models. TALISMAN, like most rental companies, charges customers for the hours of run time instead of just the number of days they have the machine. At Takeuchi, they are providing the TFM service as part of their initial, two-year, 2,000-hour warranty period. Once they go off warranty, TFM is an optional service. Today, Takeuchi has 10,000+ connected machines, so even at $10 per machine per month, that would amount to an incremental $1.2 million in recurring annual revenue. If they could provide a service worth 1% of the purchase price of the machine per month, that number could easily rise to nearly $100 million annually.

Summary

There can also be hidden benefits of connected machines. In 2016, when a contractor customer in the Northeast called their dealer to report that an $80,000 piece of equipment had been stolen off a job site, the dealer simply had to look up that particular machine in the TFM system to find its exact location. TFM's map view and GPS satellite information—with 15-foot accuracy—made locating the machine an easy task. Without a connected machine, it would have been up to the police to find it because it didn't have any other tracking device. The customer and the police went out together and found it at the exact location it was shown in the system. The customer was obviously pleased with how seamlessly it all worked, and, in the end, the equipment was only stolen for the one day.

Connected machines also promise to change how products are developed. For instance, Takeuchi product development is using the data to ensure machines are being properly sized with the right amount of horsepower performance. Given they now have access to historical machine data for specific models, when the next-generation model comes out, they are able to compare data showing the average usage of a machine's total engine output.

Ultimately, connected machines will change how they are sold and serviced. As for Chris and rental companies like his, the future is also about staying connected to customers. TALISMAN Rentals is creating a mobile app that provides customers with heavy-machine-usage alerts when the machine is reaching maximum utilization, sending a service technician within 24 hours. TALISMAN customers might also receive a notification of a winter weather change and a recommendation to purchase a block heater. In the future, Chris envisions his customers logging into the app to see alerts related to equipment maintenance and what machines he has available, and just ordering them.

20

Precision Environmental Monitoring

Accidental meetings can play a role in a lot of things. Doug Seven, Group Program Manager for Microsoft's IoT mobility practice, was at a Microsoft Connect event in 2014 as a panelist when he began talking to another panelist from Skanska about monitoring and reporting environmental conditions at job sites.

Skanska is a multinational construction company based in Stockholm, Sweden and is the fifth largest construction company in the world according to *Construction Global* magazine.[3] Notable Skanska projects include London's 30 St Mary Ax building (commonly known

---

[3] *"Top 10 Construction Companies in the World". Construction Global. Retrieved 12 June 2018.*

as "The Gherkin"), University Medical Center in New Orleans, World Trade Center Transportation Hub and the Meadowland Sports Complex—home to the NFL's New York Jets and Giants and the 2014 Super Bowl.

Many of Skanska's job sites are environmentally sensitive; in other words, there are requirements that vibration, noise or airborne particulates are kept to a minimum during certain periods of time. For example, one construction project was located next to a hospital's neonatal care unit, so Skanska had to ensure that there was no jack hammering or other noisy activities that would disturb the doctors, nurses or patients at the hospital.

Figure 20.1: Traditional Jobsite Environmental Monitoring

Historically, environmental monitoring has been a low-tech, manual process that includes mounted sensors, big, red light bulbs, and an hourly check by someone walking by each monitoring station to look at sensor readings and update the numbers on a paper log sheet, as shown in Fig. 20.1. This approach has many obvious limitations, not the least of which is the inability to communicate in real time with Skanska or the customer if there are issues at the job site, such as noise being above acceptable levels. Skanska knew it could do better, and Doug and his team at Microsoft knew they could help.

Things

Skanska's initial solution called *iSite* Monitor was deployed in 2012. It allowed a construction team to monitor a range of environmental conditions such as vibration, noise, air particulates and pressure differential. It replaced pencil and paper with a network-connected device with the ability to provide real-time notification of environmental issues at the job site. In 2014, an updated version called inSite Monitor 2.0 was deployed. This new version didn't change hardware design, but rather updated the software, which included connecting to Microsoft Azure in the backend.

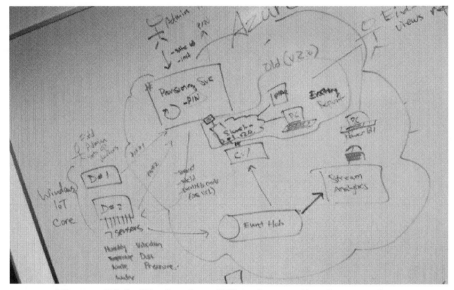

Figure 20.2: Hackathon Whiteboard Brainstorming

In 2015, Doug arranged a hackathon involving four engineers from Skanska and a group of engineers from Microsoft. The objective was to create a working proof of concept of a significantly upgraded inSite Monitor in four days, leveraging new hardware under development by Microsoft.

With a lot of duct tape and soldering, they created a prototype that replaced the existing, ruggedized, handheld sensors with smaller and less expensive sensors. These sensors included temperature, humidity, differential pressure, vibration and noise. The prototype used MinnowBoard MAX, an open hardware, embedded board that deploys the Intel Atom E38XX series system-on-chip (SOC) at its core, running Windows 10 IoT on SD card. The prototype also connected to the Azure Cloud and deployed Azure Stream Analytics for querying data streams. In addition, data visualization was done through Microsoft Power BI.

Next came the task of getting rid of the duct tape and turning the prototype into a product reliable enough to monitor real world job sites 24/7.

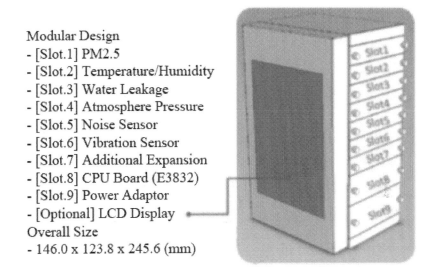

Modular Design
- [Slot.1] PM2.5
- [Slot.2] Temperature/Humidity
- [Slot.3] Water Leakage
- [Slot.4] Atmosphere Pressure
- [Slot.5] Noise Sensor
- [Slot.6] Vibration Sensor
- [Slot.7] Additional Expansion
- [Slot.8] CPU Board (E3832)
- [Slot.9] Power Adaptor
- [Optional] LCD Display
Overall Size
- 146.0 x 123.8 x 245.6 (mm)

Figure 20.3: inSite Monitor Modular Design

The next-generation inSite Monitor 3.0 has a modular design, as shown in Fig. 20.3, enabling individual sensors to be added and removed—depending on the use case requirements—without having to replace the whole device. The sensors currently available to be deployed in the field include temperature, humidity, water leakage, atmospheric pressure, noise, vibration and air particulates.

This inSite Monitor uses a custom-built board running Qualcomm's DragonBoard 410c processor. The previous 2.0 version cost $7,000–$12,000 to build, but the next-generation inSite Monitor 3.0 will be produced for around $1,200—a 90% cost savings.

On the software side it's no surprise that it runs the Windows 10 IoT Core operating system, which is a very small footprint version of the Windows OS, targeted for small-form-factor devices. Developers may write programs in .NET or JavaScript on their Windows-based computers and then deploy to computers running Windows IoT Core.

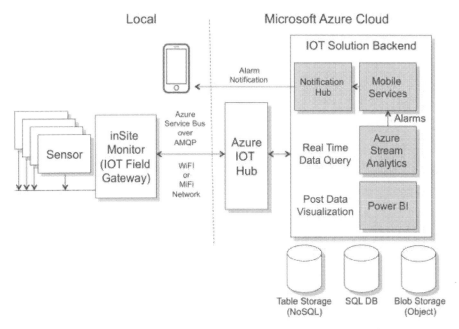

Figure 20.4: inSite Monitor Solution High-Level Architecture

Connect

As shown in Fig. 20.4, the inSite Monitor also acts as an IoT Field Gateway, connecting sensor data to the backend running in the Microsoft Azure Cloud. Network connectivity to the internet is handled via WiFi, but there are also two USB ports for connecting to a MiFi network if desired. Although each sensor is configured differently, data is typically kept on the device for 30 seconds or so and then average values are sent to the Azure Cloud.

Higher-level communications are handled via the Microsoft Azure Service Bus, which provides the messaging layer between sensors at each job site and the Azure IoT Hub running in the cloud. The Service Bus is a brokered, third-party communication mechanism, ensuring that the data is delivered even if the inSite Monitors and Azure Cloud aren't available at exactly the same time.

Data is transported using the Advanced Message Queueing Protocol (AMQP), which is an open-standard, application-layer protocol for message-oriented middleware. By using AMQP, Skanska was able to build a cross-platform, hybrid application using components built using different languages and frameworks and running on different operating systems.

Collect

In terms of storage requirements, only a few bytes of data are sent per sensor, so over a four-month period, less than 200KB of data will be stored per inSite Monitor in the field.

Once connected, sensor data is collected using Azure Table Storage, which is a NoSQL database for schemaless storage data. From there, data is processed by a cloud services worker role and transferred as structured data to an Azure SQL database. This database also stores inSite Monitor configuration data such as names and locations of sensors. Also, when an alarm goes off, a record is generated and also saved to this SQL database.

Azure Blob Storage is available to store user data and image files, although at this time no user data is being stored—only icons for images. Blob Storage is Microsoft's object storage solution for the cloud, which is optimized for storing large amounts of unstructured data.

Learn

As with most early implementations, the insight from the data that's collected is a combination of visualization and human observation. Skanska uses Microsoft's Power BI toolset for data visualization. It allows Skanska to see its data organized in different kinds of charts and graphs, which in turn allows them to see trends. For example, Skanska can graph how the temperatures have been trending over the last hour or day or seven days. Skanska can also show various things, such as current, max, min and average temperatures over the last 24 hours. In the future, Skanska plans to apply machine-learning algorithms to the stored data to search for and detect anomalies.

In order to detect when sensor values go beyond acceptable normal parameters, first an acceptable range for each sensor value is set. Data is then fed from the IoT hub into the Azure Stream Analytics engine, which is a tool for querying data streams as they're happening in real time. Azure Stream Analytics uses a programming syntax similar to Transact-SQL (T-SQL). T-SQL is a set of programming extensions from Sybase and Microsoft that add several features to the Structured Query Language. With this syntax, Skanska is able to write *SELECT* and *WHERE* statements to derive value from the data. For example, Skanska has written queries like "select where temperature is greater than X" or "select where humidity is greater than Y." In other words, as the data comes in, Skanska has written rules to detect anomalies and warning conditions in the data in real time.

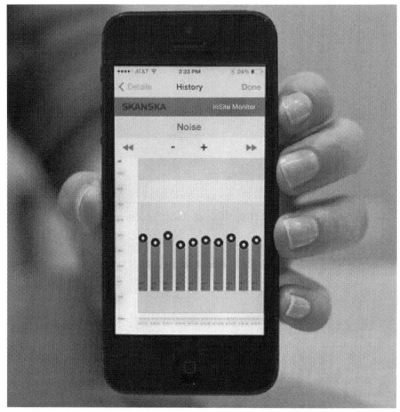

Figure 20.5: inSite Monitor Mobile App

When a threshold violation is recognized, an alarm is sent through Azure Mobile Services to the Notification Hub and out to the inSite Monitor mobile app. In addition to receiving alerts, the mobile app can retrieve real-time data so graphs can be produced, as shown in Fig. 20.5. And, given that the mobile app communicates with services running on the Azure Cloud, the app can run on both Skanska employees' and customers' mobile devices, ensuring all relevant stakeholders are always kept informed.

Do

In a typical construction project, Skanska takes all the risk of hiring contractors and doing project management. For these projects, Skanska will typically charge a flat percentage of the overall cost of the project for their services. For instance, Skanska might charge around 3%, which pays for everything included for the customer, such as IT services and support. Given this business model, the cost of the inSite Monitor is absorbed into the cost of the overall construction project, including the upfront cost for the device itself plus the monthly monitoring-service fees.

With 24/7 accessibility and alert system, the risk that unsafe environmental conditions at job sites will go undetected has been significantly reduced. Furthermore, sending real-time alerts to all stakeholders allows immediate action to be taken should an environmental issue arise at the job site. Skanska can also demonstrate compliance with both customer and government requirements and regulations.

For instance, all medical construction projects are required to maintain negative pressure to ensure airborne particulates do not drift from the project site to adjacent functioning medical operations. The inSite Monitor allows Skanska to document, validate and respond to any variations in pressure and thereby ensure 24/7 compliance. Finally, trends can be more easily identified should there be systematic issues impacting job site environmental conditions.

As an example, Skanska was contracted to build a five-story addition at San Antonio's Metropolitan Methodist Hospital (MMH). This renovation included adding two floors of care units along with endoscopy, MRI suites and emergency department support spaces.

This 85,500-square-foot, 22-month renovation took place on top of an existing operating facility. This meant that careful planning and communication with the hospital had to be a top priority. In an effort to minimize disruption to the existing operations, the project team incorporated the inSite Monitor. This allowed Skanska and MMH to monitor sensors in real time and receive notifications when a sensor was approaching a pre-set level of risk.

Summary

Environmental monitoring on a construction site is just the tip of the iceberg in terms of addressing the general challenges. Some major Asian cities are already establishing networks of sensors to monitor air quality. New York City Mayor, Bill de Blasio, announced on Earth Day 2018 that the city's air is the cleanest it's been since officials began monitoring its quality; and according to the report, air quality has been continuously improving. The mayor's goal is to achieve the "cleanest air of any large U.S. city by 2030."

This is an area where people from government, academia and the commercial side are coming together with a particular focus on how best to use low-cost, air-quality sensors to monitor cities, counties and regions. The U.S. Environmental Protection Agency has created an Air Sensor Toolbox to support communities and citizens selecting and using low-cost sensors. Commercial concerns have also emerged, such as Environsuite[4] software for environmental management and Breezometer[5], which has developed an API for displaying air quality indicators.

---

[4] www.envirosuite.com

[5] www.breezometer.com

In addition to environmental monitoring, buildings are being constructed to be smarter and more instrumented. While monitoring for smoke is important, some startups are emerging to try and improve indoor air quality. One such story begins with Aki Soudunsaari, who experienced headaches from poor indoor air quality in his school in Finland. Fast forward to today where Aki has founded Naava, a startup that builds living walls, putting to use the cleansing effect of microbes in plant roots to improve air quality. Naava removes the plant soil altogether from its walls so the air can interact with the roots directly. To further boost the purification effect, the walls are equipped with fans. Aki's advisory board includes actor Leonardo DiCaprio and spiritual guru Deepak Chopra. In Finland, Naava already has dozens of major B2B customers from business schools and corporate offices to ice hockey arenas.

Going back outside, we know that air quality, noise and vibration is just part of what will be known in a fully connected construction site. In the future, not only can the environment be instrumented, but also the people, materials and machines.

21

Precision Construction with Augmented Reality

Before a building or a space can be signed over as code compliant it has to be inspected by a building inspector. Bryan, a building inspector with thirty plus years' experience, has a well-trained eye to notice discrepancies and code violations. Over the years, his inspection routine has remained fairly consistent; he does a walkthrough with clipboard in hand, writing down code violations, such as improper window sealings or an exposed area of the fire control system, to name a few. He also completes a code inspection sheet in the form of a paper punch list.

After an inspection, Bryan manually types up his notes or transfers them onto more paper, depending on which municipality he's working for. This process is not only extremely mundane for the inspector, but also error prone, as handwriting may be illegible, the inspector may not recall exactly where he pinpointed a particular discrepancy, or there may be a miscommunication with the contractor.

Bryan says it's not an uncommon scenario to mark, say, five discrepancies in a room but only get four corrected, either because one was missed or something was corrected that didn't need to be. This wastes time and money, as unresolved problems still need to be addressed, which requires scheduling workers to return to the job to fix the issue.

Another challenge occurs with 3D building information models (BIMs). Each stage of the construction process—such as mechanical, plumbing, electrical and HVAC—has its own model, but as there is no model-design standard, conflicts can exist when the models are combined and applied. For example, a plumber might find that he can't do his work because the electrician placed wiring where the pipes are supposed to go. Resolution of this challenge today involves another manual process called "clash detection" where someone takes model segments and clashes them together in a 3D environment in an attempt to inspect and find modeling issues before building begins.

Figure 21.1: Design Tech High School

To meet these challenges when building the Design Tech High
School—a new public charter school on Oracle's Redwood City
campus—Oracle Facilities wanted to apply leading technologies and
project management to ensure on-time completion with a focus on
safety. To accomplish this, they used a combination of technologies
including augmented reality (AR) provided by DAQRI Smart
Glasses™, which provides real-time data into the Oracle IoT
Connected Worker application to enhance worker productivity and
safety, along with the Oracle Prime application for construction
project management.

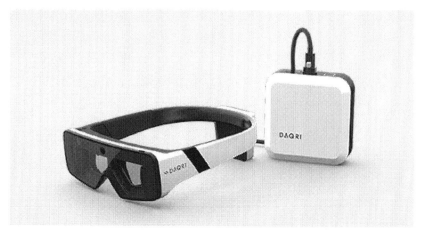

Figure 21.2: DAQRI Smart Glasses™

Things

DAQRI's augmented reality Smart Glasses™ enable workers to make better decisions in the context of what they are doing in a physical space. Smart Glasses™ can overlay and present the BIM at scale into the wearer's field of view.

The Smart Glasses™ have two components. First, the headband includes the optics and sensor packages, plus a secondary processor dedicated to the computer-vision function. The second component is a compute pack that contains the main processor, memory, storage and battery. The headband weighs 335g, while the compute pack weighs 496g. Both components also have built-in, rechargeable 5800mAh lithium ion batteries, each of which lasts about 4–6 hours with normal use.

The compute pack contains the computational capability of a high-end gaming laptop, using a 6th Generation 3Ghz Intel® Core™ m7

Processor with 8GB RAM and 64GB SSD. DAQRI uses a proprietary Visual Operating System™ and a dedicated vision-processing unit that enables movement in six degrees of freedom. In other words, where it is moving along the X, Y and Z axes and where it is rotating between X, Y and Z coordinates (pitch, yaw and roll).

The headband includes a number of cameras and sensors. Depth sensors provide information for environmental reconstruction, while other sensors track temperature, humidity, noise and location. To perform the augmented reality function, the computer overlays the BIM with what the camera sees, what the sensors pick up, where the glasses are in the physical world, and if the glasses are moving.

For a number of reasons, the devices don't include GPS. First, the devices are designed to run in GPS-denied environments. Next, GPS accuracy is only guaranteed to a few meters, which is not good enough to provide content in augmented reality. It makes a huge difference if the layered information is a few meters off the rendering of the physical space in front of the user. The level of accuracy of the DAQRI devices depends on the task requested of the device, but in general, the level of precision is within approximately one centimeter. This accuracy capability is solved by the on-board, computer-vision-based tracking, which is a proprietary DAQRI technology.

Connect

The Smart Glasses™ connect over WiFi, with IEEE standard 802.11 A/B/G/N/AC at speeds of 2.4 and 5GHz. Bluetooth® is also onboard for connecting peripherals. Sensor data, such as temperature and location, is sent to the Oracle IoT Cloud Service every 10 seconds. Building information models are downloaded, stored and operated locally both in offline and online modes, so network bandwidth is required only at the time of download.

DAQRI has a collaborative application called Show that enables the wearer to communicate with a remote expert in real time over a browser. That expert, for instance, can circle a point of interest on the browser that is then displayed to the wearer of the device. To run this application, the device requires a minimum of 350kbps of bandwidth.

All data transfer is done over HTTPS, while some customers deploy a VPN as needed. In addition, all applications run on the device are deployed through a mobile application management suite that creates a secure tunnel to the device. Applications are also individually code signed by the developers to prevent man-in-the-middle attacks, ensuring that the device doesn't receive a modified application from an untrusted third party.

Collect

Data is transferred from the Smart Glasses™ to the Oracle IoT Cloud service, which is a PaaS offering. It enables data from devices in the field in real time for analysis and integration with enterprise applications, web services, and other Oracle cloud services such as Oracle Prime and Oracle IoT Connected Worker.

Data collected includes device statistics and analytics to improve the performance of the Smart Glasses™, along with device-management data such as what applications are installed on the device and software patch levels. This data is stored indefinitely.

Sensor data is also collected in the Oracle IoT Cloud service, while camera video feeds are collected locally on the SSD. By default, DAQRI only stores sensor data required for the operation of its applications. For instance, positional information of individual tags within its Tag application is stored indefinitely.

Learn

In order to learn from this AR-provided data, Oracle Facilities began with project management by Oracle Prime, a project management application that enables team collaboration and real-time visibility across the project lifecycle. It integrates the management of project portfolios, schedules, tasks, resources, costs, field teams, documents and risk into a single platform.

Next, Oracle Facilities wanted a way to monitor the productivity and safety of the individual workers at the site. For instance, one of the requirements was that the workers couldn't rely on their hands to access information. A second requirement was to remove miscommunications and mistakes in the inspection process. Third, from a safety perspective, they wanted to ensure workers didn't end up in potentially dangerous situations, such as near extremely hot surfaces.

For this, Facilities turned to Oracle IoT Connected Worker, a cloud-based application that provides real-time visibility into worker health, location and work environment, along with better regulatory compliance. Unlike the Internet of Things that tracks connected Things, a connected *worker* is a person that has real-time, context-specific and actionable information—based on data—about himself and his physical environment. This allows him to do his job as safely and efficiently as possible.

To help accomplish this, Oracle Facilities turned to AR from DAQRI Smart Glasses™ to provide situational awareness to the device's operators, showing the right information with the right details at the right time. To make this happen, DAQRI created a suite of applications that runs in conjunction with the Smart Glasses™ and includes Show, Tag, Scan, Model and Guide, collectively known as Worksense.

Figure 21.3: Show Application

Show
The Show application allows the wearer of the Smart Glasses™ to collaborate with a second-party remote expert using a combination of video, voice and 3D annotations, as shown in Fig. 21.3. The remote

expert can see a video feed through an online browser that replicates what the wearer sees. A typical use case is to enable the remote expert to diagnose issues and provide product support.

Figure 21.4: Tag Application

Tag
The Tag application enables critical information and notes to be virtually tagged onto real-world facilities and assets that can then be managed at a glance. For instance, sensors in the Smart Glasses™ can detect if temperature levels are within, above or below the acceptable range.

In addition, required maintenance or site-inspection-discrepancy results can be tagged right onto the asset to help prioritize workloads. This way, an inspector like Bryan can digitally populate his punch list of discrepancies with precise tagging and information directly on the object in question, removing any potential miscommunication with the contractor.

These tags can be assigned to the right contractor, so there is no more guessing or re-checking that the worker is in the correct location looking at the correct discrepancy. The worker puts on the Smart Glasses™ and can see the inspector's pictures and annotations, take the corrective actions required and then confirm those actions.

In addition, all of the work is tracked by the Oracle Prime project management application and is therefore connected to the financial and resourcing aspects of the project, ensuring that nothing falls through the cracks.

Scan

The Scan application scans the environment and creates a 3D model, which is a modeled view of what the environment looks like at that point in time. The model is created and stored in the Smart Glasses™ and also streamed to an on-premise application (which is being migrated online). One application is to scan the same environment at different points in time and then programmatically show what has changed, such as progress made in the building process.

Another use allows a second party to measure to see if something will fit in the environment. For example, if the contractor has a commercial refrigerator that she wants to install in a kitchen, she can do a scan of the local environment to ensure the refrigerator will fit through all doorways leading to the kitchen, along with where she wants to install it. In this case, the Smart Glasses™ user brings in the model of the refrigerator and then attempts to "push" it through the path to where it will be installed.

Model: BIM Edition

The Model application converts high-resolution 3D BIMs from Autodesk BIM 360 Docs into immersive, full-scale walkthroughs.

Teams can compare designs to work in progress and keep the job site and the head office in sync with a fully digital workflow.

Figure 21.5: DAQRI Technology Eliminates Manual Processes

Guide
The Guide application brings instructions and reference media into the wearer's view. An example use case includes providing assembly steps to guide the wearer through a complicated task without error.

Do

Clash Detection
With the modeling application, inspectors can use the Smart Glasses™ to perform clash detection in real time, overlaying the 3D BIMs on the rendered field of view. This way the inspector can see if there are conflicts while looking through the environment. Bryan can

enter an incomplete room wearing the Smart Glasses™ and can see, for instance, if there are objects overlapping in the 3D models. Furthermore, he can see if someone installed something that is not supposed to be at that location.

Worksite Inspections

Enabling worksite inspectors to virtually tag discrepancies through DAQRI's Tag application improves both the efficiency and accuracy of inspections over traditional, manual, paperwork-filled worksite inspection processes. Oracle ran a test to see how well people could find discrepancies in the building of a large wind turbine, comparing both manual and AR-enabled processes. What they found was that discrepancies were *never* missed when using an AR digital overlay showing the location.

It's important to note that the Smart Glasses™ themselves do not point out discrepancies, but rather allow inspectors to view the map to the actual space so he or she can more easily find potential issues. If you're a senior, seasoned inspector like Bryan, you don't pride yourself on your ability to get paperwork done, but rather on your knowledge, experience and keen eye. So, removing the paperwork from the job is a huge benefit that allows Bryan to do what he does best.

Scheduling

Today it can be a challenge to schedule the different contracted teams that are involved in the building process, such as plumbing, electrical and HVAC. But with Smart Glasses™, the 3D BIM environment can be linked to a schedule provided in Oracle Prime. For example, the plumbing foreman can virtually mark his team's tasks as 'done,' which allows the electrical foreman to come in next and be confident that his team can begin work without conflict. The superintendent is also able to view the overall project status by looking at the AR environment while walking around the site where scheduled activities can be visualized.

OSHA Compliance

Another use case is OSHA compliance. Depending on the industry, there are multiple regulatory aspects that companies have to adhere to. Temperature, humidity and noise sensors on the glasses allow the superintendent to quickly make safety and health decisions with real data. There are even alerts that help them remain compliant by sending notices when data approaches certain thresholds, such as noise levels reaching 100 decibels. That superintendent can also send alerts to all the project managers through Oracle IoT Connected Worker. This results in proactive recommendations for workers to take breaks at certain intervals. Also, with the data coming in, executives are able to prove compliance using analytics to create reports that show, for example, that within the past month the temperature has gone from the medium to high range five times and the company was able to properly care for the workers in those conditions.

Worker Safety

Worker safety is also enhanced due to sensors on the Smart Glasses™ that detect if a fall occurs. In this case, data is transmitted to the Oracle IoT Connected Worker application that notifies the superintendent. In addition, using the DAQRI Guide application, augmented reality can also be used to train people in the safe and proper operation of machinery or tools.

Resource Management

Another use case is the ability to do resource management with sensors assigned to each worker. For instance, let's say there are five drywall workers who are supposed to come to work today. Sensors on each worker's device are associated with and preconfigured based on the type of worker. When the worker checks in with the Smart Glasses™, the worker-tagged data is sent to Oracle IoT Cloud Service and makes the information visible to users via Oracle IoT Connected Worker. This way the construction company can see that, say, only four of the five drywall workers came to work and will call the superintendent on the worksite to go over and adjust the job plan accordingly through Oracle Prime.

Summary

It shouldn't be surprising that the facilities department of one of the leading Silicon Valley tech companies would be very forward thinking in terms of how to apply technology to increase construction productivity and safety. However, it's another thing to transition from vision and desire to implementation and execution.

Oracle Facilities saw the opportunity to apply augmented reality to improve the productivity and safety for the building of the Design Tech High School. For their part, the teams at DAQRI, Oracle Prime and Oracle IoT Connected Worker made all the magic happen. Ultimately, no worker was hurt and construction stayed on schedule. And as an extra bonus, now worksite inspectors like Bryan can throw their pen and paper away and spend more of their time doing what they do best—discovering and reporting on discrepancies so fixes can be made and projects can stay on schedule.

22

Precision Robotic Masonry

F.A. Wilhelm Construction Company Inc. (Wilhelm) established its
roots as a masonry contractor in 1923 in Indianapolis, Indiana. Since
then the company has completed more than 8,000 projects in Indiana
and the Midwest. These projects range from parking structures to
buildings such as the NCAA Headquarters, the JW Marriott and
Cummins buildings in Indianapolis, and the Belterra Casino in
Florence, Indiana.

Mike Berrisford started his career with Wilhelm in 1996 as a first-
year apprentice bricklayer. Today he manages the 150+ person
masonry division and oversees all field operations. With his 22 years
in the industry, Mike has come to deeply understand the pain points
and challenges facing construction masonry companies.

One big challenge is the lack of qualified people coming into the construction business, and even fewer coming in to be bricklayers. Today, masonry is populated with an aging workforce at a time when maintaining a high level of quality requires top-notch craftsmanship and work ethic—much more talent than the industry is able to hire.

Wilhelm turns very few applicants away due to the high demand for labor, and as a union contractor, the wages are attractive. However, want ads tend to draw a lot of under-qualified people—many of whom lack a high-school education—so unfortunately, when it comes time to read a tape measure or follow a blueprint, they quickly don't measure up. In fact, nearly two-thirds of bricklaying contractors say they are struggling to find workers, according to a survey by the National Association of Home Builders.[6]

To address these and other issues in the masonry field, Nathan Podkaminer and Scott Peters started Construction Robotics (CR) in 2007 with the goal of advancing construction through the use of robotics and automation. The company's flagship product is the semi-automated mason known as SAM. A typical mason will lay between 350 and 550 bricks in an eight-hour day, whereas SAM lays 350 bricks per *hour*, while never needing to stop for a coffee or bathroom break.

---

[6] Share of Builders Reporting Labor Shortages Rises Again
http://eyeonhousing.org/2017/08/share-of-builders-reporting-labor-shortages-rises-again/

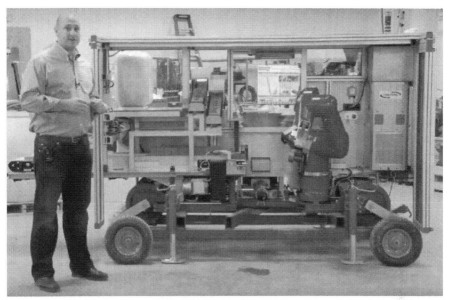

Figure 22.1: SAM100

Things

The SAM100 was the first commercially available bricklaying robot for onsite masonry construction. It was launched in February 2015 at World of Concrete in Las Vegas where it won the Industry Choice Award for most innovative product. The newest version, the SAM100 OS 2.0, debuted at World of Concrete in January 2017. SAM is a collaborative robot designed to work with the help of trained masons; it relies on one mason to operate it, a tender to load it with bricks and mortar, and another mason to secure wall ties, remove excess mortar and lay bricks in corners or other challenging areas.

Components and Sensors
SAM's basic components include a large robotic arm with multiple joints, a laser eye that detects depths and distances required to place

each brick, a pair of story poles at the left and right of the work area, a CAM (computer-aided manufacturing)-generated design for mapping the job and a tablet-based control panel.

SAM includes several sensors that measure and track velocity, incline angles, orientation, outside and enclosure temperature, humidity, run hours, GPS, safety and more. For instance, SAM measures the slump and quality of mortar being applied. All data generated is time stamped to the millisecond.

Using SAM
Before starting work on a wall, masons first use digital maps of the architectural blueprint to take measurements of the work area before programming SAM accordingly.

Coursing is done with laser story poles that communicate the course line to SAM. A course is a layer of the same bricks running horizontally in a wall. Without SAM, this is done manually using string.

Course - Horizontal Layer of Brick

Figure 22.2: Definitions

The ideal wall for SAM to build is one that is long, straight and flat. At this point, doing detailed and intricate walls with window returns or piers is difficult. That said, SAM can adapt to deviations between plans and actual, as-built conditions, as well as adjust the plan before starting work.

For instance, with non-robot-built walls, head joints—the vertical mortar joint between bricks (shown in Fig. 22.2)—will oftentimes be off by the time the end of the wall is being built. This is due to minor errors in the earlier measurements, as the slightest variation of head joint width will compound the longer the wall. For instance, if a wall's head joints are supposed to be precisely three eighths of an inch but end up being a fraction larger, this small error will compound, potentially making the last head joints an inch or larger.

SAM can see this before starting the wall and shrink or extend the head joints to make up for the variance. To accomplish this, SAM measures the dimensions of every single brick that goes into the wall. With this data, SAM is able to differentiate between brick sizes and brick types in addition to all the configurations and colors they come in. With each brick, SAM knows exactly where it goes and if everything is at the same plane, projected or recessed and by how much.

Considering that SAM is a *semi*-automated robot, it still needs the skill and assistance of trained masons working alongside it to ensure quality and accuracy of certain aspects of the job. For instance, SAM picks up every brick by three points (two on the back and one on the front), but if one of those points hits a bump or piece of debris on the brick, SAM doesn't know that, so it still presses on the three points assuming they are the same every time. In this case, it could twist the brick by as much as a quarter of an inch. Given this, SAM requires two masons to follow along and clean up the mortar while fixing any twisted bricks as the robot goes along the wall.

Running SAM does require special training, and companies have to choose who will be setting up and running SAM on job sites. For SAM's debut job, Mike at Wilhelm chose to train a couple computer-minded crewmen who weren't yet foreman but had been in the trade long enough to understand the ins and outs of laying brick.

Admittedly, finding good bricklayers within a company who are not only savvy enough to learn how to program SAM but also interested in learning something new can be a challenge.

Figure 22.3: SAM Robot at Work

Connect

All data collected by SAM is uploaded over LTE in real time to CR's own, self-managed private cloud running in an outsourced datacenter.

Every five minutes, CR transmits all activity since the last upload, which includes information on each and every brick placed. This data includes length, width and height coordinates, outside temperature, humidity, mortar slump, mortar applied to which bricks, which brick in wall, location of brick, course of brick, time and date each brick went into the wall, and how long it has been since the previous brick was placed. In addition, system information is also uploaded to CR's servers. All data transferred is encrypted.

Collect

Data is stored in a SQL database running on the hosted database server. After six months, data is archived indefinitely.

The datacenter is protected by a firewall. In addition, no one has access to the database directly. CR uses a front-end application that interacts with the data and presents it to users based on a user-access system administered by the web server.

Learn

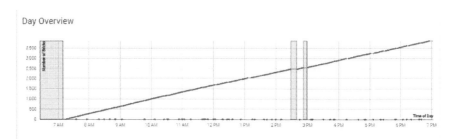

Day Overview

Figure 22.4: Day Overview Dashboard

Start	End	Total Time	Brick Count	Productivity	Machine Utilization
7:13 AM	6:55 PM	11:41	3851	329 bph	86.47%
6:25 AM	7:03 PM	12:38	4101	325 bph	80.05%

Figure 22.5: Two-Day Summary

Construction Robotics provides an application so every contractor who signs up for an account can gain access to the data from their jobs. The application is tiered and goes from a high-level overview all the way down to a specific day for a specific job. Supervisors can look at the data in real time and see things like performance trends, average bricks laid per hour or per day, peak production times, downtime, and more. For instance, in Fig. 22.4 we see the number of bricks laid during a single day and in Fig. 22.5 we see a summary over a two-day period. In addition, workers can upload pictures and notes, which are also tracked.

It's interesting to note that, generally speaking, the current mindset in construction is that the status of a project can be understood through pictures. However, there is no real data stored in a picture. Unless you examine the photo and count every brick, you can't know how many bricks are actually in a wall, let alone exactly how long it took to put them there. With SAM, data from every single brick and all of its sensors is tracked and learned from, allowing the customer to see who was working with the machine, who was mixing the mortar, the temperature outside, whether or not it was raining, and much more.

Often at the end of a job, data is downloaded to create presentations on SAM's performance. This data helps customers understand the value of using SAM because it usually shows how production for a first-time SAM job increases steadily over the course of the project due to the learning curve in the first couple weeks as workers get used to using and working with SAM. From that data, the contractor can see how future projects with SAM will be even more productive, assuming the workers won't have that learning curve a second time. Using analytics to see trends in this data is what truly allows for improvement in performance and efficiency.

Figure 22.6: SAM at Work on a Tall Building

Do

When Mike first met with the Construction Robotics team to see how SAM worked he was impressed and decided to try it out. After a trial project, Wilhelm became the first contractor in the world to own a SAM robot and has used SAM on many projects to date. As SAM is geared towards flat, straight walls, Wilhelm continues to look for those types of (easy to find) jobs, as he sees the benefits of using the robot.

The biggest benefit to using SAM is that it is relentless; it doesn't require bathroom or lunch breaks and doesn't get distracted by texts and phone calls. SAM keeps working as long as it's full of fuel, mortar and brick, dramatically increasing productivity and efficiency. This isn't to say that the crew has less to do now, however. Human labor is still needed to mount insulation sheets, screw in brick anchors, retrieve materials and monitor quality. But now the crew can do those things *while* SAM is laying brick—at a rate of about one every eight seconds.

Using SAM also reduces the crew size. A job that once took five bricklayers and two laborers now takes two bricklayers and one laborer, saving customers more than 50% on labor costs. At first glance, one might think there is a concern that SAM and other construction robot technology will eliminate the need for a mason in the future, but CR disagrees. Even large construction companies like Wilhelm understand that the older generation of masons is retiring and fewer young folks are entering the industry, especially those with intent to do traditional, physical labor. Therefore, the ability to remain highly productive with fewer people is a good thing. In addition, working with construction technology like SAM is more attractive to younger generations.

Figure 22.7: SAM and Mason Working Together

Bricklaying is a manual, repetitive and very physically demanding job. SAM takes an immense amount of that physical labor and repetitive motion away from crew members, enabling them to work safer with less fatigue and a lower risk of injury. CR has found that using SAM reduces lifting aspects of the job by more than 80%, which helps to increase the overall health and safety of the masons.

The quality of wall alignment also improves. At the end of the day, using SAM results in as good a product or better than you can get with only human labor. For instance, SAM is exceptionally good at lining bricks up vertically. Head joints done by human labor will always drift laterally due to human variation, but with SAM's laser guides and sensors measuring and adjusting for vibrations or wind on the scaffold, vertical lines are kept perfectly straight.

SAM also provides customers with valuable insights and analytics for estimating and scheduling future projects. CR is able to tell a customer what to expect for performance on any particular job with different aspects of a wall system thanks to all of the known information such as brick types and number of windows. This information takes the guesswork out of estimating future projects, giving the customer a lot more confidence to schedule jobs and line up labor.

Figure 22.8: A Brick Wall Built by SAM

Summary

As Wilhelm is an early adopter of new technologies, Mike has seen the pros and cons of using new methods and machines in the construction field. He believes that as SAM evolves and the team at Construction Robotics continues to improve the technology to do more complex projects, SAM's big splash into masonry will morph into steady waves that truly change the industry. SAM is growing in popularity with every project, having installed more than one million bricks, and worked in more than 19 states with more than 148 masons on more than 29 different construction sites. People like Mike remain cheerleaders for SAM and the innovative company, saying: "The group of people at Construction Robotics is just amazing."

23

Summary – Solutions

If you've been in Silicon Valley in the past several years you've probably heard the phrase, "software is eating the world," coined by Marc Andreessen, which could now be amended to "software and data are eating the world." As a manufacturer of any industrial or enterprise Thing (e.g., machine, asset, device), you'd be wise to take note of this phrase. Companies like GE and Bosch have already embraced this view and started investing significant amounts of money in the ability to connect, collect and learn from their machines. In the last several chapters, you've seen examples of what manufacturers of machines are doing and how it's beginning to change their business models. In time, it might be difficult to see the difference between a software company and a machine company.

So, as a builder of construction Things, what are some of the steps necessary to begin the digital transformation of your business?

First, you have to invest. That doesn't just mean buying software from a supplier and having them implement it; instead, you must invest in the talent. Dr. Chou did a talk for some of the senior managers at GE titled, *What's the Difference between Hardware and Software?* In the talk he highlighted two differences. With hardware, people tend to think that having a larger team to build a jet engine, for example, is better than having a smaller team. In software it's the opposite. This idea is illustrated by the story of a meeting Dr. Chou had with Oracle's Larry Ellison, Safra Catz and Jeff Henley. During the meeting, Jeff (CFO at the time), using a few salty expletives, asked Larry, "Why is the Salesforce.com CRM product so much better when we have 500 developers and they only have 50?" Larry replied, "That's precisely the answer." Your investment in talent does not have to be 50 or 500, but you should at least start with the *right* five.

Of course, you're also going to invest in building machines with more sensors, more local computing and flexible communications. Consider the framework we've outlined and think about what your high- and low-level connection architecture is going to be. How will you collect the data? What approaches will you use to learn from that data? How much will you buy? How much will you build? Should you sole-source with one supplier or build a stack unique to your business?

Again, what you've done is necessary but not sufficient. All of this technology is meaningless without answering how you're going to apply it and what the business benefit is. In previous chapters we discussed three major business models for manufacturers. First, connect the machine and provide a service contract. When Jack Welch was at the helm, GE made a major shift to this model; it's worked for them and also helped build some of the largest software companies.

Second, if you're connected to the machine, you can also provide assisted services because you know what's happening on the machine and, more importantly, have seen what works across hundreds or thousands of similar machines, allowing you to provide information on how to maintain or optimize the performance, availability and security of these machines. And of course, if you can provide advice, you can also implement those changes and begin to offer machines as a service and move to a highly profitable, recurring-revenue model.

There are challenges to doing this, the least of which is being held hostage to the past. While many machines and devices have software, it has always been a necessary evil to the main player on the stage: the people. The November 2015 issue of *The Economist* eluded to this by saying, "The principal sticking-point in making this digital leap is often cultural […]."

As an enterprise that makes machines, integrating mechanical engineers with software engineers is not an easy task. Mechanical engineers focus on physical products and think about development lifecycles of three to five years; they know there's no stopping production once it starts and what is produced has to be deployed in the field and support a lifecycle of decades. On the other hand, the software engineers are thinking about minimum viable product, perpetual beta and updating services daily. As a start, you might follow what GE has done in naming a chief digital officer, in their case, a person with equal executive footing to the leaders of GE Power, Aviation and more.

The opportunities are large for both existing players and new entrants. As the role of software and analytic technology grows, the potential exists to build the next generation of machines in a totally different way. You don't need to look any further than the car you drive to wonder if your next one will be from Ford or Apple.

Service Economy

Estimates vary, but 85–90% of the U.S. economy is a service economy. While a much lower percentage, Mexico and China are moving more and more toward becoming service economies themselves. So what is a service economy? Officially, it includes every company that is not making something (manufacturing) or growing something (agriculture). The service economy includes industries like healthcare, retail, financial services, education, transportation, utilities and, of course, construction.

So what is service? Is service answering the phone nicely from Bangalore? Is it flipping burgers at McDonald's? The simple answer is *no*. Service is the delivery of information that is personal and relevant to you. That could be the hotel concierge telling you where the best Szechwan Chinese restaurant in walking distance is, or your doctor telling you that based on your genome and lifestyle you should be on Lipitor. Service is information that is personal and relevant to you.

In the world of construction, "you" could be the machine operator, the field service engineer, the warranty manager, the parts manager, the CEO of the construction company or the engineering team designing the next-generation fork lift. What's important to remember is service is information that is personal and relevant to all of these stakeholders.

Digital Transformation
If service is information, then start by finding all of it and making it personal and relevant to people. On a construction site, that might include the executive staff, site supervisor and procurement manager. We implore you to not be held hostage by the SQL monster, but what does that mean?

Let's say it's the late 90s and we have a bunch of SQL engineers in a room to present them with a brilliant business idea: we are going to index the consumer internet and we're going to monetize it with ads—we're going to be billionaires! Just guess what the SQL engineers would do?

First, they will design a master, global data schema to index all the information on the planet. Then they will write ETL and data-cleansing tools to import all that information into this master schema. Finally, they are going to write reports on, say, the best place to camp in France or great places to eat in San Francisco.

If you are remotely technical you are probably laughing right now and thinking how completely idiotic that is. But it can be argued that every city and business out there continues to try to adopt this mechanism to deliver any kind of information that might be personal and relevant.

Therefore, we would counsel you to consider that the term *consumerization of IT* does not apply to the question of whether or not you should use Facebook at work; instead, it speaks to the question of how to leverage these technologies to deliver personal and relevant information to the contractor executive, field foreman, procurement manager and operator of a rental agency.

Next, you should buy and rent smart machines and connect them, whether they are skid steers, scissor lifts or track loaders. Allow the machine data to be used by the manufacturers to assist or implement higher performance, availability or security of the machines. The manufacturer is building precision machines because they are leveraging software and data across hundreds of thousands of machines. Precision machines deliver higher quality service, lower cost consumables (e.g., fuel) and lower cost of servicing the machines. As the contractors and rental agencies of the future leverage these precision construction machines, anyone using these machines will benefit.

Challenges
The Internet of Things heightens existing concerns about cyber security and introduces new risks, multiplying the normal risks associated with any data communication. Each device increases the "surface area" available for breaches, and interoperability expands their potential scope. Every node is a potential entry point and interconnection can spread the damage. Moreover, the consequences of compromised IoT systems that control the physical world could be catastrophic; a compromised medical monitor could be a matter of life or death, and a hacker attack on a smart-grid system could potentially turn off power to millions of households and businesses, creating massive economic harm and threats to health and safety. Again, we're going to need to invest in innovative ways to protect these systems and engineer it into the products.

Also, any digital transformation of a manufacturer, rental agency or contractor will require people. We've already quoted *The Economist*, as well as highlighted how the biggest inhibitor will be the organization itself. In the end, leadership will be essential.

Finally, as our population grows and we put more demands on the physical world, we're going to need to move toward becoming a precision planet; it makes no sense to waste water, fertilizer, pharmaceuticals and energy. It is widely recognized that global growth opportunities for the next several decades will be in Latin America, Southeast Asia and Africa. According to the UN DESA report, "World Population Prospects: The 2015 Revision," Africa is expected to account for more than half of the world's population growth between 2015 and 2050. The population of Nigeria is projected to surpass that of the U.S. by about 2050, at which point it would become the third most populous country in the world.

On a broader scale, developing economies need infrastructure: construction, power, water, agriculture, transportation, healthcare and telecommunications. Will this infrastructure be built the 20th century way? Or, as we've seen in China, will developing economies leapfrog and move to 21st century cellular technology and never use landlines?

Africa may hold the keys to our next evolution. Electric power in the U.S. is generated in large oil or coal-fired plants and distributed in a hierarchical manner. But in the modern world, you'd never do it that way; you'd take advantage of solar, wind and hydroelectric generation, all geographically distributed. Furthermore, you'd build some storage mechanisms, which our traditional power grids don't have. Essentially, the entire control of this power grid would be distributed and enabled by computers that not only have access to information about the wind turbine (generated every six seconds), but also the current weather and demand. And you may even move to generating direct current without ever going to alternating current, as even lighting is moving to direct current. In short, this future power system would look nothing like what we have today.

Building this in the U.S. today would be nearly impossible. In Africa, it would be the only way; you'd skip telephone lines and move directly to cellular. Africa holds the potential of skipping ahead to the next-generation farm, water treatment plant or hospital, unencumbered by the infrastructure and rules of the past. Perhaps you will become part of this evolution and build power plants, hospitals, schools, water treatment plants and more with this new level of insight enabled by our connected, smart machines. We certainly hope so.

Glossary of Terms

19-foot scissor lift – A sustainable option for your raised platform needs

3G – Short for *third generation*; is the third generation of mobile telecommunications technology

Accelerometer – An instrument for measuring acceleration, typically that of an automobile, ship, aircraft or spacecraft, or that involved in the vibration of a machine, building or other structure

ACID – Atomicity, Consistency, Isolation, Durability: a set of properties that guarantee that database transactions are processed reliably. In the context of databases, a single logical operation on the data is called a transaction

AMQP – Advanced Message Queueing Protocol

AR – Augmented reality

ARMA – Autoregressive Models: Provide a simple but effective form of dynamic machine-learning algorithm; when a value from a time series is regressed on previous values from that same time series

Assisted Services – Rather than making and implementing the decisions to improve the security, availability, performance and change, you offer advice and let the owner of the product manage the changes

AWS – Amazon Web Services

BIM – Building Information Model

BLE – Bluetooth Low Energy

Boom lift – A boom lift is a type of aerial lift that provides much greater flexibility than a scissor lift because it's supported by a hydraulic arm that is capable of maneuvering around obstacles.

Boot – When the machine powers up and is the first software to run

CAM – Computer-Aided Manufacturing

CAN – A Controller Area Network (CAN bus) is a robust vehicle bus standard designed to allow microcontrollers and devices to communicate with each other in applications without a host computer.

Classification – The prediction problem if the outputs are discrete values (predictive model is known as a classifier)

Cluster – A collection of input data vectors that is similar according to some metric

Clustering – A set of techniques for discovering patterns or "clusters" within input data

CMU – Communications Management Unit

Combine harvester – Also simply called a *combine*; a machine that harvests grain crops

CPU – Central Processing Unit

CRISP cycle – Based around exploration, it iterates on approaches and strategy rather than on software designs

CRM – Customer Relationship Management

DMZ – Demilitarized Zones: May be used to protect the process control system from the internet and the business network

DPF – Diesel Particulate Filter

Duty cycle – A duty cycle is the fraction of one period in which a signal or system is active. Duty cycle is commonly expressed as a percentage or ratio. A period is the time it takes for a signal to complete an on-and-off cycle.

Dynamic machine learning – Concerned with the analysis of sequence or temporal data for which he standard independence assumptions inherent in many machine-learning algorithms do not apply

EDA – Exploratory Data Analysis: Initial steps of a machine-learning project

Encryption – The process of encoding messages or information in such a way that only authorized parties can read it

ERP – Enterprise Resource Planning

ETL – Extraction, Transformation and Loading: The process of extracting data from source systems and bringing it into a data warehouse

Eventual consistency – Database changes are eventually propagated to all nodes (typically within milliseconds) so queries for data might not return updated data immediately

Feature engineering – Task of determining a suitable representation of the raw input data that maximizes the performance of a machine-learning model

Feature vector – Resulting data vector used as the input to the model

Firewall – A network security system that monitors and controls the incoming and outgoing network traffic based on predetermined security rules

Fixed-size vector – A number of input-data values

Gene or DNA sequencer – An instrument used to determine the sequence or order of the four bases — G (guanine), C (cytosine), A (adenine) and T (thymine) — from any plant or animal cell

GDSP – Global Data Services Platform

Geo-fencing – A virtual perimeter for a real-world geographic area

Global SIM – Provides a single means (SKU) for products to be distributed worldwide.

GPRS – General Packet Radio Service; a data service on 2G or 3G cellular networks

GPS – Global Positioning System

GUI – Graphical User Interface: A tool used to help formulate queries

Gyroscope – A spinning wheel or disc in which the axis of rotation is free to assume any orientation by itself; a sensor that can provide orientation information but with greater precision

Hardening – Having all good software and no bad software

HDFS – Hadoop Distributed File System: A Java-based file system that provides scalable and reliable data storage designed to span large clusters of commodity servers

Health monitoring or condition monitoring – Tasked with building an algorithm that can predict if an engine is operating normally or, alternatively, operating in a novel or abnormal way that may indicate a problem within the engine

History mapping – A capability that allows customers to see any machine's last ten moves, displaying a marker on a mapping application that shows equipment make, model and number, along with position recorded by latitude and longitude.

Historians – Time-series databases

HR – Human Resources

HSPA – High Speed Packet Access

HVAC – Heating, Ventilating and Air Conditioning

IDE – Integrated Development Environment: Software that provides comprehensive facilities to computer programmers for software development

Interrupt latency – In computing, interrupt latency is the time that elapses from when an interrupt is generated to when the source of the interrupt is serviced.

IoP – Internet of People

IoT – Internet of Things

ISDN – Integrated Services for Digital Network

ISO 11992 – A CAN-based vehicle bus standard by the heavy duty truck industry. It is used for communication between the tractor and one or more trailers.

ISO 15143-2 – Standard used for communications from the machine to the internet

J1939 – Standard that defines the recommended practice to be used for communication and diagnostics among vehicle components.

JVM – Java Virtual Machine

KPIs – Derived sensors (e.g., daily production rate)

Labeled dataset – An input/output pair consisting of the input vector together with the desired output value (label)

Line-of-sight range – From antenna A you can see antenna B

LOCOCOMM – A CMU applicable to both GE and non-GE locomotives

LoRaWAN – Long Range Wide Area Network: protocol specification built on top of the LoRa technology that enables low power, wide area communication between remote sensors and gateways connected to the network.

LPWAN – Low Power Wide Area Network: Designed for wireless, battery powered Things

Machine data – The state of the blood analyzer or the gene sequencer

Magnetometer – Measurement instrument used for two general purposes: to measure the magnetization of a magnetic material like a ferromagnet, or to measure the strength and, in some cases, the direction of the magnetic field at a point in space

Mapping – Takes the form of a mathematical function, which is governed by a set of parameters (or weights)

MapReduce – A programming model and an associated implementation for processing and generating large data sets with a parallel, distributed algorithm on a cluster

Microcontroller – A small computer on a single integrated circuit. In modern terminology it is similar to, but less sophisticated than, a system on a chip

Middleware – The software that connects software components or enterprise applications. The software layer that lies between the operating system and the applications on each side of a distributed computer network. Typically, it supports complex, distributed business software applications.

MiFi – A brand name used to describe a wireless router that acts as mobile Wi-Fi hotspot

ML – Machine Learning

Moore's Law – The observation that the number of transistors in a dense integrated circuit doubles about every two years.

Nomic data – Data that describes what the machine is measuring, such as properties of soil or blood

Normality model – Test new input data against this model and evaluate the probability that the data is indicative of the system operating normally (i.e., that the input data could have been *generated* by the normality model with high probability)

NoSQL – Originally referring to "non SQL" or "non relational" database; provides a mechanism for storage and retrieval of data that is modeled in means other than the tabular relations used in relational databases

Novelty or Anomaly detection – The identification of new or unknown data that a machine learning system has not been trained with and was not previously aware of, with the help of either statistical or machine learning based approaches

OEMs – Original equipment manufacturers

OLAP – Online Analytical Processing: Performs multidimensional analysis of business data and provides the capability for complex calculations, trend analysis and sophisticated data modeling

One-factor authentication – A process for securing access to a given system, such as a network or website, that identifies the party requesting access through only one category of credentials

OPC – Open Platform Communications

OS – Operating System

OSHA – Occupational Safety and Health Administration

OSI – Open Systems Interconnection: Conceptual model that characterizes and standardizes the communication functions of a telecommunication or computing system, without regard to their underlying internal structure and technology

OSISoft's PI system – One of the earliest time-series databases

Output values – Estimating one or more desired quantities of interest

Packaging – A major discipline within the field of electronic engineering that includes a wide variety of technologies

Patch – A Piece of software designed to update a computer's software

Pedometer – A sensor used to count the number of steps the user has taken

PII – Personally Identifiable Information

PLC – Programmable Logic Controller

Predictive model – Provides a mapping from the input-data vector to the desired output value(s)

Product-as-a-Service – Manufacturer retains ownership and takes full responsibility for the security, availability, performance and change of the product in return for a recurring charge

Query – A specific request for a subset of data or for statistics about data, formulated in a technical language and posted to a database system

RDBM – Relational Database Management System

Regression – The prediction problem if the outputs are continuous values (predictive model is known as regression model)

RISC – Reduced-Instruction Set Computer

RTOS – A real-time operating system; an operating system intended to serve time-critical applications

SaaS – Software-as-a-Service

SAE J1939 – The bus standard used for communication and diagnostics among vehicle components

Segregate machine data – Data that describes the state of the machine such as its operating temperature and battery level

Service and Support – Product sales bundled with warranty or service contracts

SiP – System-in-a-Package; alternative to SoC

SKU – A single means for products to be distributed worldwide

Slap Track device – A small basic unit that attaches to a machine to provide location and an estimate of run hours based on vibrations

SoC – System-on-a-Chip; one of the packaging technologies used in high volume

SPL – Search Processing Language

SQL – Structured Query Language: A special-purpose programming language

Supervised learning – A predictive model that maps an input pattern to a desired output value

Tag – A data point for each input sensor

Thread-switching latency – the time needed by the operating system to switch the CPU to run another thread. ... There is no virtual memory switching required in a thread switch, unlike a process switch.

Time Series – A series of data points indexed (or listed or graphed) in time order. Most commonly, a time series is a sequence taken at successive equally spaced points in time

TLS – Transport Layer Security: Cryptographic protocols designed to provide communications security over a network; frequently referred to as 'SSL'

Transact-SQL (T-SQL) – A set of programming extensions from Sybase and Microsoft that add several features to SQL

Two-pipe approach – Describes both machine information and *nomic* information. For example, a gene sequencer may have sensor information describing the reagent or voltage level of the machine (machine information) but also deliver genomic information — your DNA sequence.

UDP broadcast/multicast protocol – Further increases the volume of network traffic

UHF – Ultra high frequency cellular option capable of 1–12 miles, depending on the terrain

Unsupervised learning – The finding of clusters in a set of input data that does not require any output values to be present in the dataset

VoIP – Voice over IP

VPN – Virtual Private Network

Workflow or process management – Software used to orchestrate a step-by-step sequence of actions

Index of Vendors

A

AdONE   74

AGCO   48, 124

Amazon Web Services (AWS) 5, 69, 72, 74, 160, 181, 252

Amtel   22

Amtrak 112

Appareo   48

Apple 21-22, 89, 246

Arduino 22

ARIMA   86

AspenTech   65

ARM   11, 19, 22

Arrayent   47, 65

Association of Equipment Management Professionals (AEMP)   26, 168

Association of Equipment Manufacturers (AEM)   26

Atomiton   24

Autodesk 223

Axeda   47

Azure Cloud   202, 205-6, 208

Ayla Networks 47, 65

B
Baseplan
BigTable
Blackbaud   102, 109
Bobcat   173
Bosch   243

C
Cassandra 65
CAT   120, 172
Caterpillar   173
Cisco   53, 74, 105, 181
ColdLight 16
Concur   102
Constant Contact 7
Construction Robotics   230, 235-6, 238-41
Creo 16
Cummins   34

D
DAQRI   38-39, 76, 216-220, 226
Dealertrack 102

E
eBay 112
Elasticsearch   68
EMC 74
Environmental Protection Agency (EPA)   33, 210
eTrade 7

F

F.A. Wilhelm Construction Company Inc. 229-30, 234, 238-9, 241
Facebook   53, 65, 247
Fitbit 127
Ford   246

G

GE (General Electric)   12-14, 17, 54, 65, 107-8, 243-5, 257
GE Power   245
Google   53, 66, 89, 109, 112

H

Hadoop 13, 66
Hive   67
Honeywell 121, 173

I

IBM's Maximo   77, 122
Intel   22, 38, 40, 54, 216
Lyft 109

J

JLG   31, 54, 74, 116-17, 120, 172, 177-178, 180-5
John Deere 120, 172
JP Morgan Chase 14

K

Komatsu   120, 172

L

Lecida   89

LOCOCOMM 54, 257

M
Mahout 67
MAPICS 74
MapReduce 66-67
Maximo 113, 122
McCrometer 44
Metropolitan Methodist Hospital (MMH) 209
Microsoft 6, 25, 35, 40, 77, 98, 102, 109, 201-2, 207, 262
Microsoft Azure Cloud 53, 75, 201, 205
MongoDB 68

N
Naava 211
NetSuite 7, 102

O
Oomnitza 113
OpenTSDB
Oracle 6, 25, 76-7, 102, 106-7, 224
ORBCOMM 31, 74, 180
Orange 56
OSHA 259
OSIsoft 65

P
PayPal 7
PeopleSoft 6, 102
Pig 67
Pivotal 77
PTC 14, 16-17, 47, 89

PyTorch 89

Q
Qualcomm 35, 203

S
Salesforce   7, 102, 109, 122
Samsung 21
SanDisk   62
SAP   6, 102, 106
Schneider Electric Company 14, 65
Semtech Corporation 57
ServiceMax 89
ServiceNow 122
Sharp 21
ShoreTel   191
Siebel   6, 102, 122
Siemens 25
Silver Spring Networks 47
Skanska   35, 53, 75, 97-8, 199-202, 206-7, 209-10
Splunk   67-8, 71
Stanford University 98, 127
SuccessFactors   7, 102
Sun Microsystems   107
Sybase   98, 207, 262

T
Tableau
Takeuchi 30, 75, 95-7, 116, 118, 188, 191, 193-5
Taleo   7, 102
TALISMAN Rentals 187-8, 195
Tata Communications   56-7

Telstra 57
TensorFlow 89
Teradata 77
Tesla 106
ThingWorx 16
Tsinghua University 5

U
Uber   109, 112
Uniquid   49
United Rentals 31-2, 51, 72, 76, 92-4, 118-20, 136, 139-41, 145, 151, 153-5, 157-9, 161-5

V
Veeva   102
Vestas 76
VMware   25
Vodafone   52

W
WebEx   7
Windchill 16
Wind River   24
Workday   109

Y
YotaScale   69-70
YouTube 53

Z
ZTR Control Systems 30, 32, 48, 75, 141-2, 144, 160, 190-1

Index of Terms

A

ACID properties   63
AEMP (Association of Equipment Management Professionals)   26, 168
AMQP (Advanced Message Queueing Protocol)   135, 206, 251
augmented reality (AR)   8, 37-9, 76, 134, 213, 215-17, 220, 224, 226, 251
AWS (Amazon Web Services)   5, 69, 72, 74, 160, 181, 252, 263

B

battery level   31-2, 142, 160, 180, 260
BIMs (building information models)   37-9, 214, 216-17, 223-4, 252
boom lift   24, 30, 94, 171, 179, 252
Building Information Model   37, 214, 217, 252

C

cloud service   102, 122, 127

cloud service providers   69, 128

CMU (Communications Management Unit)   54, 252, 257

construction companies, largest   35, 167, 199

construction machines, next-generation   134

construction project's costs   94, 171, 175

CRM (customer relationship management)   6-7, 12, 127, 253

D

DAQRI Smart Glasses   38, 215-16, 220

databases, relational   63, 258

Depth sensors   39, 217

DESA (Department of Economic and Social Affairs)   268

digital transformation   105-6, 110, 243, 247-8

Disconnected Services   106

duct tape   202-3

Dynamic Machine Learning   85, 253

E

ECM (Electronic Control Module)   33

Environmental Protection Agency (EPA)   33, 210

ERP (enterprise resource planning)   6, 12, 107, 122, 253

ERP software   7, 74

F

forklifts   49, 103-4, 119, 153

fuel   111, 115, 120, 154, 165, 238, 248

G

geo-fencing   31, 94, 119, 150, 154, 180, 254

H

Hadoop   66-7, 71, 265
HID cards   122, 174
HMMs (Hidden Markov Models)   86
hour meters   171-2

I

IAM (Integrated Access Management)   49
Increasing Machine Utilization   118
inSite Monitor   35, 53, 201, 205-6, 209-10
Internet of People (IoP)   5-6, 24, 49, 122, 126, 256
IoP middleware   123-4
IoT Framework   9-10, 12, 47

J

Java Virtual Machine (JVM)   23, 256

L

LPWAN (low-power wide-area networks)   56, 257

M

machine data   59, 67, 98, 124, 136, 144, 175, 182, 194, 248, 257
machine learning   8, 86, 88, 98, 127, 129, 258
machine-learning algorithms   79, 86, 98, 207, 253
machine-learning model   85, 87-8, 254
machine-learning project   84, 86, 88, 253
machines, connecting   41, 111, 117, 195
maintenance   72, 89, 104, 116-17, 140, 152, 155, 159, 183, 188, 191, 194-5
MAPICS   74, 265
mapping   36, 81, 148, 191, 232, 257, 260
Metropolitan Methodist Hospital (MMH)   209-10, 266
Microsoft Azure Service Bus   205
Microsoft SQL server database   73, 75, 170, 191
monitoring, environmental   35, 134, 201, 210-11

N

NoSQL   11, 61, 63-4, 67-8, 71-2, 144, 160, 258

O

OLAP (Online Analytical Processing)   80, 259
Open Systems Interconnection (OSI)   41, 259
operator-performance tracking   121, 173
operator's console   97, 194
Oracle cloud services   76, 218
Oracle IoT Cloud   76, 218-19
Oracle IoT Connected Worker   219, 225-6
ownership, total cost of   77, 117, 183

P

Packaged IoP Applications   122
pedometer   21, 259
PLCs (programmable logic controllers)   25, 57-8, 260
Precision Contractor   55, 73-4, 118, 120, 167-71, 173-5
Precision Framework   133-4
precision machines   8, 17, 103-5, 113, 116, 129, 248
Precision Service   111-12
prediction problem   81, 252, 260
predictive model   79, 81, 84, 252, 260-1
Product-as-a-Service   109, 260

R

RDBMS   62
rental agencies   8, 31, 116-17, 136-7, 183, 247-8
rental companies   117, 177, 182-4, 188, 196
RTOS (real-time operating system)   23-4, 260

S

SAM   36-7, 230-5, 237-41
Satellite-based Augmentation System (SBAS)   52, 190
Search Processing Language (SPL)   68, 261
Secure Sockets Layer (SSL)   53, 262
security   4, 6, 11, 24, 48-9, 59, 69, 103, 107-9, 123-4, 128, 168, 245,
248, 252
security appliances   58
sensor data, stores   76, 219
service economy   246
services

better 8, 103, 165

fleet-management 118

higher quality 161, 248

web 26, 76, 218

SiP (system in package) 28, 261

Skanska 35, 53, 75, 97-8, 199-202, 206-7, 209-10

Slap Track Device 32, 141-2, 160

SoC (system-on-chip) 28, 202, 261

Society of Automotive Engineers (SAE) 26

software, bad 25, 48, 128, 255

software-as-a-service 7, 260

Software-Defined Machine 106

software maintenance 12, 101

SQL 61-4, 72, 80, 98, 135, 144, 160, 261-2

SSD 38, 76, 217, 219

SSL (Secure Sockets Layer) 53, 262

Supervised-learning algorithms 79, 82

T

T-SQL 98, 207, 262

Takeuchi 30, 75, 95-6, 116, 118, 188, 191, 193-5, 267

TFM (Takeuchi Fleet Management) 30, 75, 116, 118, 187, 190, 192, 194-5

time series 64, 85, 251, 261

time-series data 64-5, 85, 108

Total Control 52, 72, 93, 118-20, 140-1, 144-5, 147-8, 151-5, 160-1, 164-5

U

UR (United Rentals) 31-2, 51, 72, 76, 92-4, 118-20, 136, 139-41, 145, 151, 153-5, 157-9, 161-5, 268

V

vibrations 32, 34-5, 97, 142, 160, 200-3, 211, 240, 251, 261

W

WiFi 43-4, 53-5, 135, 169, 180, 205, 217

Z

Zigbee 43, 53, 55, 169

37303833R00178

Made in the USA
Columbia, SC
28 November 2018